ECHOES OF MY SOUL

Also by Robert K. Tanenbaum

Fiction

Tragic
Bad Faith
Outrage
Betrayed
Capture
Escape
Malice
Counterplay
Fury
Hoax
Resolved
Absolute Rage
Enemy Within
True Justice
Act of Revenge
Reckless Endangerment
Irresistible Impulse
Falsely Accused
Corruption of Blood
Justice Denied
Material Witness
Reversible Error
Immoral Certainty
Depraved Indifference
No Lesser Plea

Nonfiction

The Piano Teacher: The True Story of a Psychotic Killer
Badge of the Assassin

ECHOES OF MY SOUL

Robert K. Tanenbaum

KENSINGTON BOOKS
http://www.kensingtonbooks.com

KENSINGTON BOOKS are published by

Kensington Publishing Corp.
119 West 40th Street
New York, NY 10018

All Kensington titles, imprints and distributed lines are available at special quantity discounts for bulk purchases for sales promotion, premiums, fund-raising, educational or institutional use.

Special book excerpts or customized printings can also be created to fit specific needs. For details, write or phone the office of the Kensington Special Sales Manager: Kensington Publishing Corp., 119 West 40th Street, New York, NY, 10018. Attn. Special Sales Department. Phone: 1-800-221-2647.

Kensington and the K logo Reg. U.S. Pat. & TM Off.

Library of Congress Card Catalogue Number: 2013930669

ISBN-13: 978-0-7582-8535-5
ISBN-10: 0-7582-8535-3

First Printing: June 2013

10 9 8 7 6 5 4 3 2 1

Printed in the United States of America

To DA Frank Hogan, Mel Glass and John Keenan—courageous souls who ran a Ministry of Justice reflecting the moral and spiritual essence of American exceptionalism.
To Henry Robbins, who always believed and first published and edited Badge of the Assassin *and put me on this path.*
To the blessings in my life: Patti, Rachael, Roger, Billy and my brother, Bill.
To the loving memory of Reina Tanenbaum, my sister, truly an angel.

ECHOES
OF MY
SOUL

CHAPTER 1

August 28, 1963, Upper East Side

In the west courtyard there was a line of windows, which were in the kitchens of individual apartments, and there was a vent, which protruded from a brick wall and led into each of the kitchens. On the second and third floor, the protruding vent was positioned between the window of the kitchen and the window of the service stairwell.

Agitated, the baby-faced drug addict noticed an open window on the third floor and lit a cigarette. Then he paced nervously in the courtyard, taking a long, pensive drag. He studied the prospect—at first casually, then with determination. Sunlight dappled over that portion of the building, so he couldn't get a clear view inside the slender opening. He squinted and lifted his hand to shade his eyes, but he still wasn't sure if anyone was home—not that the presence of the occupant, particularly if she was attractive, would be a deterrent to his penchant for home burglary. The thief just liked to know what he was getting himself into. Already a career criminal, just shy of twenty, he had become the go-to suspect whenever a burglary went down on the Upper East Side of Manhattan. City cops estimated that he was responsible for approximately one hundred unlawful break-ins, in a losing attempt to gain money necessary to support his drug habit. In fact, just two months earlier, he was paroled from Elmira Reformatory for "good behavior."

It was muggy out. While temperatures hadn't yet peaked, it felt as if the concrete sidewalks were sizzling. And even though it was a hot summer day, goose bumps formed along his spine as he pressed a paper bag underneath his arm. It contained a pair of pink rubber gloves from the five-and-ten store on East Eighty-sixth Street. He took a few heavy breaths to work up his nerve. *Get it together,* he said to himself, *it's time.* He stamped out the cigarette, wiped his brow, then walked toward the basement entrance of the building on 57 East Eighty-eighth Street.

Katherine Olsen stepped from the shower in time to hear the doorbell. She draped a robe around her slender figure and rushed to the door, where she accepted a package from Bloomingdale's. Katherine, "Kate" to her friends, called out to one of her roommates, Emily, asking if she wanted to try out the new towels. The bathroom door sprang open. A skinny girl, with thick, dark glasses, wearing a green printed shirt and dark skirt, stood barefoot. Her legs were crossed in a kind of flighty, ballerina stance, and the handle of a blue toothbrush jutted out from her mouth. She muttered "no thanks" and darted back to a white porcelain sink, where she spit her toothpaste out and studied her complexion in the mirror.

"You're missing out, Emily Hoffert!" Katherine called from the kitchen. "You could've been the first to test them."

Emily blotted her forehead with a tissue and sighed. *Pasty, pale skin, and it's the end of the summer,* she thought, rubbing some rouge into her cheeks. She could hear the sound of Kate's new beige heels marching about in the kitchen. She eventually joined her for coffee. Beads of perspiration were already forming on both girls' foreheads. Emily sat down and pressed her index finger to the bridge of her glasses, attempting to prevent them from sliding down her nose. She poured some milk in her coffee and used both hands to lift her cup to her unpainted lips. Katherine, with a beehive of chocolate brown hair, held a compact in front of her face and pressed her nose. She complained of the heat and how she wished they could afford air-conditioning. Emily complained that she had to return her friend's car, up in the Bronx, where her own green Fiat was parked. Then she said, pointing around the corner, "Hey—does she sleep all day or what?"

Kate rolled her eyes and grinned widely. She pressed her finger to her lips, forming a shushing motion. Emily was referring to their third roommate, twenty-one-year-old Janice Wylie. Emily dubbed her "the blond bombshell," based on her bouffant of blond hair and stints in amateur-theater groups. As it was, Emily had only been living in their 57 East Eighty-eighth Street digs for the month. Kate, her roommate at Smith College, was the one who helped orchestrate the temporary arrangement (Emily was moving downtown with her friend Susan in a few days). In all the moving, they hadn't really had a chance to gossip.

"Do I look like her mother to you?"

"Kate," Emily whispered, "did you—did you know she sleeps in the nude?"

Snapping her compact closed, Katherine answered matter-of-factly, "If I had her figure, I would, too. Besides, it's horribly hot."

Just then the phone rang, reverberating throughout the apartment. Katherine jumped up and marched over to the living room, the heels of her shoes making a loud clomping noise as she went. She heard Janice call out faintly that she got it.

While chewing on a piece of toast, Emily said, "Say—I thought she was going to be in Washington today for the march?"

Katherine walked back to the kitchen and grabbed the garbage.

"Just a sec—I always forget to do this first thing."

3

Kate walked over to a door in the kitchen that led out into the service stairway. On the stairwell sat an orange garbage pail. She tossed the garbage in the pail and came back inside.

"Her ride fell through at the last minute, apparently. That's probably *Newsweek* on the phone. I think she was trying to get some hours in today."

Kate sat back down and took a sip of coffee. "I wish I could've gone," she added.

"No kidding. Is it going to be on the tube?"

"Apparently. In fact, it might be on already."

"Oh, Kate, let's catch a minute of it, shall we?"

The girls grabbed their coffee and headed into the living room, where Emily flicked on the television. Katherine glanced at her watch and chose to stand rather than sit, as it was close to nine-thirty and she had to get downtown to the Time-Life Building, where she worked as a researcher. In black-and-white images, they watched a sea of people walking along, many with signs. A voice interrupted, announcing that upward of two hundred thousand people were expected to march from the Washington Monument to the Lincoln Memorial. Emily sat on a folding chair and inched it closer to the screen.

"Is that wild or what?" she called out excitedly.

Katherine nodded, grabbing her purse and keys off the end table beside the couch. As curious as she was about the March on Washington, she was more concerned with getting downtown to the office.

"Want to walk out together?" she asked, setting her coffee cup down.

Emily nodded and reached for her car keys. She reluctantly turned the knob on the TV until the screen went gray. She remained frozen for a moment, just long enough to see her reflection in the rounded screen. She blinked and pouted her lips. She could hear Katherine tapping her foot impatiently in the doorway. She slowly lifted her purse strap onto her shoulder; then she leapt from her chair and raced Katherine out the door.

Sometime before noon, after having returned from the Bronx with her green Fiat, Emily reentered the apartment and heard strange noises coming from her bedroom. She wandered down the hall in her brown sandals and, distractedly, turned to walk into her room. She saw Janice, naked and panting, with a man on top of her, unbuttoning his pants. Emily stood in the doorway, studying the scene for a moment, before managing to say, albeit under her breath, "Janice?"

Instantly the man turned, frantically climbing off the bed. Emily looked from the man to Janice and back to the man. He was young, possibly her age; he moved toward her intensely—a pair of rubber gloves covering both hands.

"Janice?" she echoed again.

Janice sat up in bed, pulling a sheet up to cover her body. Emily noticed her eyes were puffy from crying.

"Just do what he says, Em—"

Emily remained paralyzed and dumbstruck in the doorway. Her glasses stayed perched on her nose while her eyes widened in fear. The man grabbed her hair and pulled her into the room. He ripped the sheet from Janice and pushed her onto the bed. Then he grabbed Emily by the back of her neck and threw her next to Janice, tying them together with pieces of fabric he tore from the bedsheets. As Janice and Emily shook and whimpered, he went to the kitchen. The girls remained whisper silent. Tears rolled down Janice's cheeks as Emily continued to ask her, as faintly as she could, what had happened. Janice shrugged her shoulders and continued opening her mouth, as if to speak, but nothing came. From Emily's vantage point, she could see a jar of Noxzema open and tossed on the floor. She flinched and tried to reassure Janice that it was almost over. As it was, she thought—

she hoped—he might be leaving. Although Emily had only managed to catch a glimpse of him, the man appeared flustered. The girls shook, back to back, on the cool white sheets. Emily could hear Janice reciting the Lord's Prayer.

Then they heard his footsteps gaining. Janice sniffled and began whimpering. Emily tightened the muscles in her legs. He returned with a strange, mischievous grin on his face. Through quickened breaths, Emily managed to say, between gasps of air, that she was trying to remember his face so that she could report him to the police.

The man paused, his smile fading. He asked her to repeat what she had said, but Emily lost her nerve. She opened her mouth, but only a faint whisper came out. The man tore Emily's glasses from her face. She felt the violence in him as his hand grazed her cheek. Tears welled up in her eyes and she tried to tell herself to be brave. He stepped back into the hallway. Emily blinked her eyes repeatedly, but the room was now a blur.

The second hand on the clock ticked quietly from the bathroom, and they could hear water drip from the spigot across the hall. Emily listened to his breathing in the hallway. Janice whispered to Emily that she didn't want to die; Emily told her she wasn't going to. The siren of an ambulance could be heard in the distance as it made its way down Fifth Avenue. The fan on the bedside table oscillated, left to right, then right to left, and back. It whirred gently, blowing Emily's bangs into her eyes.

In the hallway the man paced, up to the living room and back down again. Emily heard a loud thud, as if something was thrown against the wall. A moment passed and she heard it again. The breathing thickened, the footsteps grew louder, until their pace quickened to a horrifying gallop. Janice shivered and cried out. Emily began to sob.

Now, in a frenzy, sweating profusely, with two soda bottles, one in each hand, he moved catlike toward the girls. Then Janice let out a bloodcurdling scream. He lifted the bottle in his left hand and smashed it over her head several times. With the other bottle, he mercilessly struck Emily repeatedly about the head and face. Instinctively, Emily reached out her hands defensively. As she was losing consciousness, words came to her, simple and wholly desperate, which she uttered: "Please, please . . . don't hurt me anymore." But it was too late—the killing had begun.

With knives grabbed from the kitchen, the man stabbed and stabbed, amid the desperate cries and pleadings. He stabbed so many times, in fact, that he broke the nib of one of the knives slicing into the left side of Emily's jaw. He broke another, attempting to thrust a knife into her back. At some point the girls' bodies fell to the hard floor with a lifeless thump. And after what seemed an endless, maddening amount of time, he stopped. The sight of his work and the smell of the blood made him feel nauseous. He stood up and set down two of the bloody, broken knives on a nearby radiator. Then he searched the closet for a shirt he might be able to change into. To his surprise he found a man's brown jacket and a few white T-shirts. Not wanting to stain the clothing with his bloody gloves, he stepped into the bathroom across the hall, dropping the third knife in the sink. He turned on the shower and undressed quickly, trying to avoid staining his clothes any worse. He peeled off the bloody rubber gloves and tossed them in the shower. The killer scrubbed his body swiftly, meticulously. He dried off and re-dressed in the bedroom, throwing on the white T-shirt and brown sports coat, along with his own bloodstained pants. He threw the gloves and his shirt in a brown paper bag. Then he rifled through Emily's wallet, which was resting on the bureau, and ripped off thirty dollars. Finally, just as the heat of the day was breathing in, he charged down the hall, escaping through the service stair door.

An eerie silence followed, interrupted only by the distant cacophony of cars honking and city buses rolling by. Broken glass was everywhere; blood dripped from the walls and soaked into the floors. The clock radio beside the bed remained curiously frozen at 10:37 *A.M.* The window shade in the bedroom had flecks of blood on it and billowed forward in the breeze, only to snap back, beating the sill. Emily Hoffert lay on the floor, faceup. Her head was turned toward the window, with tears that had streamed down her face. She was nearly decapitated; her glasses rested on the bed, covered in blood. Beside her, in the heat of midday, rested Janice Wylie. She was naked, and her head was also turned toward the window. Her abdomen had been completely disemboweled. It was Wednesday, August 28, 1963.

At six-thirty in the evening, she immediately called out for Janice. Kate Olsen received a call earlier in the day from Janice's mother, who mentioned that *Newsweek* called inquiring as to Janice's whereabouts. This didn't exactly surprise her, as Janice was known to be a bit capricious, but it did surprise Kate that her roommate hadn't bothered keeping her in the loop. Kate stepped into the apartment, closing the door behind her.

"Janice? Janice, are you back there?"

Kate reached up and slipped off her shoes, rubbing a callus that had formed on the back of her right heel. She noticed the door to the hall closet was open; a raincoat, with a hanger intact, rested across its threshold.

"Janice," she called out again—loudly, boldly—"darling, where *are* you?"

The apartment was oddly silent, but for the hum of a fan oscillating somewhere in the back. As she passed the dining room on the left, she noticed the service doorway was open. This sent a chill down her spine and she paused, catching her breath. Kate shifted her gaze back to the long, narrow hallway, which led to the bedrooms. She noticed the door to her bedroom was open and light spilled out into the hall. She paused at the doorway and peered in.

It appeared to be ransacked. The sheets were off Janice's bed and a pile of clothing lay in a heap on the floor. Drawers were open. Things had been pulled off the top shelf of Kate's closet. Kate glanced back and noticed a light on in the bathroom across the hall. She stepped out of the bedroom and peeked her head into the bathroom, where she called out Janice's name yet again. This time her voice held a slight quaver. On the floor of the bathroom was a moist sheet, which Kate dared not touch. The shower curtain was pulled open and the taps were dripping. She took a step back, shifting her gaze to the sink, where she noticed a kitchen knife lying on top of the drain. *That can't be,* she thought. *No, that simply can't be there.* Kate's eyes remained locked on the knife just long enough to register what appeared to be blood on the tip.

"Janice?" she whispered.

Kate rushed down the hall to the living room, where she telephoned her date, Tim Krupa, who said he would be over immediately. Next she dialed Janice's parents, who lived two short blocks away, at 55 East Eighty-sixth Street. When Kate described the condition of the apartment to Janice's father, Max Wylie advised her to call the police immediately. Kate called the police, reporting a burglary; then she went out the front door of the apartment and rode the elevator down to the lobby. She wasn't really sure where she was going or why. . . . She just needed to go.

She rushed out of the building and paced under the awning. She squinted quizzically toward Madison Avenue and then toward Park. Maybe Janice got a ride to Washington, after all, she reassured herself, stepping back inside. *Let her be in Washington,* she prayed. *Let her be away.* The night doorman stood near the elevator and she asked him, in passing, if he'd seen Janice. He asked, which of her roommates was Janice?

"The blond one," Kate replied anxiously. "Emily's the one with the glasses, and you don't need to remember her, anyhow. She's moving out tomorrow." The doorman wrinkled his brow and then answered slowly but confidently that he had not seen Janice. He added that he would ask the morning doorman if he had any recollection. Kate thanked him and walked away.

The elevator door opened and she stepped in, traveling back to the third floor, where she reentered apartment 3C. Just then, the doorbell rang and she rushed to answer it. Mr. and Mrs. Wylie entered the apartment; both were pale-faced. Max Wylie immediately advised the two women to remain in the living room while he searched the apartment. Although his demeanor seemed overly calm, Kate noticed Mr. Wylie's hands were shaking, too, as he set out down the long hallway.

He reached his daughter's room first, which appeared ransacked, just as Katherine had described it. He stepped back into the hallway and paused. He heard his wife, Lambert, call out, but he couldn't distinguish what she said.

"Stay in the living room," he shouted, "and don't touch anything!"

He noticed a hem of light coming from the second bedroom. The door was ajar, four or five inches. He took a few paces and wedged the door open with his foot and knee. He was able to see a bed with various things piled on top of it. Max froze. The entire room was in disarray. His lips began to quiver. The drawers of a bureau opposite the bed were all pulled open, to varying degrees, and the floor was strewn with personal objects. He stood just inside the doorway for quite some time, slowly grasping the frenzied state of things: the plaid hatbox and black purse tossed on the bed; the hangers, papers and wrapping paper littering the floor; the lopsided state of the lace curtains on the two windows at the far side of the room. Nothing, it seemed, was where it should have been. There was also a frightful, metallic, nauseating smell that permeated the room. Then he recognized that the mattress by the window was covered in what appeared to be blood. And to his horror, he caught sight of something—something unnatural and unfathomable. His throat went dry.

Max let out an aching sigh and felt his knees buckle beneath him. There was something on the other side of the far bed, something beyond those bloody sheets. He was afraid to cross the room. "Oh, sweet Jesus," he whimpered, "no." And yet he had to face whatever repulsion lurked there. Ultimately this was his duty, he felt. Max allowed a few more seconds to pass as he composed himself. Then, with every ounce of courage in him, he inched his way around the second bed to a confined space by the window. There, on the cold floor, lay his daughter and Emily Hoffert. The sight before him was so drastically nightmarish, so ghastly, that in his own lifetime, he would never manage to erase the image from his mind.

With all his might, he tried not to focus on the gore. Instead, he saw a blue wool blanket near Emily's knees and instinctively pulled it, gently, over the bodies, covering the girls as much as he could. His hands shook and he gasped for air. "My baby," he moaned softly, "oh, my little girl." Max rested the palm of his hand on the blanket near the top, where Janice's head was. Then he withdrew slowly, trying to avoid stepping on the shards of glass that dotted the floor. He took a few deep breaths, attempting to compose himself, and headed out of the room, back down the hallway toward the living room.

He saw his wife, seated just as he'd instructed, with her arms folded. Still, his whole body seared in pain. He saw Kate, wide-eyed and frantic. He tried to find the words he needed to impart. His whole body ached and burned—he could hardly contain his own singular fright and startling grief.

"Max? What did you find?" his wife asked, reaching her hands out desperately. Her voice cracked, and he could see the tears welling up in her eyes. Mr. Wylie stood before the two women, white-faced; his arms were to his sides, but his hands were lifted, palms down, as if to say, *Calm down, let's just stay calm.*

"Dear," he managed in a throaty voice, "I need you to be strong now."

Mrs. Wylie's face turned white; tears dripped from her eyes and she blinked several times. Max went to her, fell to the ground and grabbed her hands. He looked over to Kate Olsen, feeling his own tears coming on swiftly. For a split second, he managed to smile at Kate reassuringly, but this grin crumbled beneath his trembling lips. He turned back to his wife. Barely audible, now overcome with the unforgivable reality, he muttered, "It's all horribly frightful."

Sobbing, he continued to speak. "Janice is gone—Emily too. . . ."

Mrs. Wylie blinked again and asked, " 'Gone'? My God, Max—gone where?"

"Dear—"

Max closed his eyes—tight—feeling the gushing tears coursing down his face.

"Dear," he repeated, looking at her squarely, "the girls have been murdered. . . . Janice is dead."

CHAPTER 2

Eight months later, Brownsville section, Brooklyn

At a few minutes before one in the morning, on Wednesday, April 22, 1964, police officer Tommy Micelli was already into his shift, just shy of an hour. Micelli, a member of the New York Police Department (NYPD) for a little over three years, was assigned to the Seventy-third Precinct, which encompassed most of the Brownsville section, an area comparable in crime conditions to Harlem. On that early morning, he had a foot post during a midnight-to-eight-*A.M.* tour. It had been raining when he first came on duty, and now, an hour later, the rain had stopped. There was still a moistness in the air when Micelli walked to a police call box near Sutter Avenue and Chester Street. It was time for him to call the police house or "make the ring," as it was referred to. He picked up the phone and called in. Then he began walking west on Sutter Avenue toward Bristol Street. Almost immediately he noticed the figures of a man and woman on Bristol Street some two hundred feet from him. The man appeared to be pushing the woman into an alleyway.

Officer Micelli immediately sprang to action. He came racing toward them in the dark, his shoes hitting the pavement quick and hard. He shined his flashlight in the alley and saw a young man leap out and sprint along Sutter Avenue.

"Hey!" cried out Micelli, who was heavily winded from running so fast. He grabbed the .38-caliber revolver out of his holster and sped up.

"*Hey!* This is the police! Stop where you are and raise your hands!"

Micelli's pace quickened more as he stretched to close the gap between him and the assailant. His legs burned. They rounded a corner west onto Hopkinson Avenue. Micelli lost his footing and tripped, almost landing hands first on the ground. He fell half a block behind. The assailant rushed forward, like a bullet. Micelli pushed off again, his shoes grazing the loose gravel. He fired off a few shots and called out once again. His breath was steady and shallow. When the suspect reached Amboy Street, which was one block west of Hopkinson, he turned to his right and disappeared. By this time there were a few police cars on the scene, with sirens blaring. Red and blue lights flashed everywhere. Micelli ran another two blocks before realizing he'd lost sight of him. The even sound of footsteps, too, was all but gone. Micelli could hardly see beneath the muted streetlamps of Brownsville and the pulsing lights from police cars behind him. Reluctantly, he slowed to a halt. He bent over, placing his hands on his thighs, desperate to catch his breath. He listened to the sound of his own wheezing.

Micelli gazed out into the desolate city night. The street resembled a ghost town. There were just a few neon lights shining in front of stores, and siren lights reflecting in puddles. After a few moments, he steadied himself, watching as his fellow officers sprinted past him. He stuffed his gun back in its holster and shuffled back to the scene of the crime.

She couldn't stop shaking. Alma Estrada glanced down at her white nursing shoes, splashed with mud. She whimpered. The sidewalk was damp and moist from earlier rain showers. A street-lamp flickered two blocks ahead and the glaring sirens blinded her. Alma was petite, and just twenty years old. She cried out for her husband, who had raced down from their apartment and wrapped his arms around her. Over and over he asked her what had happened, but she could barely speak. Her face went white and she gasped for air, managing a few words here and there. As the moments ticked by, more officers began assembling around Alma, each with a notebook and pen in his hand, ready to scratch anything down, any detail at all. Officer Micelli edged his way into the semicircle as Alma accepted a handkerchief and blew her nose. With the slightest hesitation, she began relaying the details of her story.

First, she said, she heard—or thought she heard—a noise. Her heart skipped a beat and she lengthened her stride. But with each stride she took, the sound behind her steadied. Footsteps, she said. She was sure then. They were firm; they were cold; they were metallic. She rounded a corner, her legs stretching out in front of her. Her heartbeat quickened and perspiration formed on her brow. She told the officers of how she tried to convince herself it was all in her head—that she was working herself up for nothing. And yet there was no mistaking the footsteps be-hind her: they were real *and* moving.

The sea of officers took note as she crossed her hands over her heart and tried to explain how the adrenaline coursed through her body. The men nodded, all heads down and scribbling. Next she clumsily attempted to illustrate how she then began to jog. Alma stood there, beneath the streetlamp, attempting to run in place. Instead, she appeared as if she was limping awkwardly. Her purse dangled on her wrist. She explained to the officers how as curious as she was to look behind her at her chaser, she did not turn around. She was terrified. She told them that she moved to the center of the street until, finally, he reached her and thrust his arm around her throat and pressed a sharp metal object against her neck.

Alma Estrada drew her neck toward the officers and explained, in hurried syllables, "He whispered in my ear, 'I'm going to rape and kill you.'"

Then she held her arms to her neck, in a choking manner, and described how her assailant dragged her into a nearby alley. Her glasses fell off, and somewhere in there she must've screamed. Alma had already furnished a pencil, a button and some thread when officers first arrived. She insisted that the pencil was what the attacker had held to her throat and that the button and thread came directly from the assailant's jacket. After a few more minutes, the assembled crowd began dispersing. Alma's husband wrapped his arms around her. After the police finished their questions, the couple disappeared into their apartment building.

Officer Tommy Micelli did not give up easily. After hearing Alma Estrada's teary-eyed, if not frenzied, side of the story, he decided to retrace his steps. It was just after dawn when Micelli wandered down Sutter Avenue a second time. He was hopeful, if not entirely convinced, that one of his shots hit the attacker. *Surely, there might be a trace of blood,* he thought as he surveyed the gray asphalt carefully. Micelli paced up and down a two-block radius along Sutter Avenue. A gust of wind swept by. There was a chill in the air and some light misting—all common symptoms of early spring in New York.

Tracing his steps, it wasn't long before he found himself on the corner of Hopkinson Avenue. He thought there was a chance he had wounded the assailant, but his search for bloodstains on the pavement proved fruitless. Through the window of a Laundromat, he noticed a young black man sitting by himself. Given the time of day, the individual seemed out of place to Micelli. *Better safe than sorry,* Micelli reasoned, deciding to walk in and ask a few questions.

Upon sight of this young teenager, Officer Micelli was immediately distracted by his skin. He was sitting in a metal chair by one of the dryers; his arms were folded at his chest. He peered up at Micelli as he entered. While the structure of his face was agreeable enough, and his large, squinting brown eyes seemed pleasant and unassuming, the young man's cheeks and forehead were covered with open acne sores. In trying not to stare, Micelli focused on the kid's dark hair, cut short without sideburns.

"Good morning," Micelli said, nodding at him. He noticed the young man had just uncrossed his arms, placing them nervously at his sides.

"Hello, sir."

"It's a bit early for laundry, don't you think?"

The kid flinched and answered slowly. "I was just . . . waiting inside, from the cold. My brother is coming by and we're going to walk to work."

"I see. Well, it *is* very cold outside."

Micelli paused for a moment, trying to read the boy's unsure expression. Then he added, "And where do you work, if you don't mind my asking?"

He went on to tell Micelli that his name was George Whitmore Jr., and that he had a job at the local salt-packing plant. Micelli wrote everything down on a scrap of paper, which he peeled off from inside his jacket, even though he doubted it would prove useful. He then thanked the young man and, having never sat down, headed toward the door.

"Think it's gonna be a rainy one today, Mr. Whitman," Micelli said.

"Whitmore," George corrected.

"Whitmore. Sorry about that, kid."

Micelli had just opened the door; the doorbell had just chimed, when George Whitmore Jr. sat up out of his seat, the metal chair squealing on the linoleum floor. Micelli turned back.

"Sir," George said timidly, "I know why you're asking me these questions."

Micelli let go of the door and reentered the Laundromat.

"Oh? Why?"

"It's about that fellow the police were chasing last night. What was the shooting all about?"

Micelli walked slowly over to George. There was something particularly curious about George Whitmore Jr.—or, at least, Officer Micelli thought as much. For one thing, young black kids rarely spoke to police in Brownsville, particularly where crime was concerned. And then there was the hour—it was just seven in the morning, and Micelli found himself engaged in polite small talk with a teenager, haphazardly placed at a Laundromat mere blocks from where Mrs. Estrada was attacked. Micelli began to study George more carefully now: his slight gait, his long fingers, his awkward squinting gaze. As he did, Micelli briefly outlined the attack on Alma Estrada; to which, Whitmore added, almost interrupting, "How low can some people get. I saw the cops chasing the man down Sutter Avenue, and they were shooting at him. He went into a building on Amboy Street. I can show you where, exactly, if you like."

Micelli was intrigued. Rather than question him further, he followed Whitmore a block west on Sutter Avenue, where George pointed to a tenement building the attacker had hidden in. As suspect as Whitmore was, or perhaps should have been, Micelli found him to be surprisingly innocuous and genuinely helpful. From a nearby call box, Micelli reached the precinct's street sergeant, where he reported Whitmore's information. Soon enough, another car arrived.

Whitmore seemed eager when the squad car roared up beside him on Sutter Avenue, its driver window rolled down to reveal a bloated, ruddy face, with a dark, bushy mustache. Micelli and Whitmore were standing on the sidewalk, just outside the Laundromat, when the sergeant leaned out the window to speak to

George. The odor of a cigar wafted from the car as George stepped over to it.

"Between you and me," the man said, "it's against the law not to tell the police where a guy went to, when we're looking for him."

George stared at the sergeant, perplexed. "But I—"

Micelli squeezed Whitmore on the shoulder in reassurance and walked up to the sergeant's window. The two men spoke momentarily in low voices. Then the sergeant revved his engine, told Micelli he'd be in touch and drove off, leaving a trail of exhaust. "Well, hell, thanks a lot, Whitmen," Micelli remarked, reaching out to shake George's hand.

"Whitmore," George corrected again, shaking his hand. Then he added, "Is it okay if I head off now?"

Micelli smiled and waved him off lightheartedly. He watched, amused, as Whitmore lifted his hand awkwardly in an attempt to return a variation of Micelli's good-natured gesture. Instead of a wave, Whitmore's hand managed an ungainly, cheery slap of the thigh. Then his slight figure disappeared around the corner of the Laundromat. *That's a good kid*, Micelli thought, walking away into the clear morning.

In the early 1960s, a detective within the Seventy-third Precinct in Brownsville, Brooklyn, was overtaxed with heavy caseloads—upward of six hundred—not to mention the reputation of working at the toughest station house in New York City. In addition to the average caseload, in April 1964, two detectives, Louie Ayala and Joseph "Joe" DiPrima, were caught trying to solve another brutal murder—that of Mrs. Minnie Edmonds, a forty-six-year-old woman who was stabbed to death in an alleyway, exactly one block east of where the Alma Estrada assault had taken place. Mrs. Edmonds's clothing was disarranged in a manner indicating sexual assault. Her attack had also taken place in the early hours of the morning. As was true for most homicides out of Brownsville, the Edmonds case certainly didn't send ripples through the heart of Gotham as the Wylie-Hoffert case inevitably did. But for the people of Brownsville and its police, this murder was highly disturbing. For Ayala and DiPrima, they had exhausted all their leads. Still, neither was about to give up; both were first-grade detectives, the highest detective mark available. Ayala had been on the force for sixteen years, while DiPrima had put in over twenty-seven. The two detectives worked well as a team, tirelessly following over ninety leads, but to no avail.

Then, on Wednesday morning, April 22, 1964, Officer Tommy Micelli walked into the Seventy-third Precinct station house and handed over his information on Alma Estrada. Joe DiPrima glanced at the file and passed it on to Ayala. He looked at Micelli head-on.

"You got a witness?"

Micelli raised his eyebrows and wiped his brow with a handkerchief. "The kid said he saw him clear as day."

Ayala ran his fingers through his cropped, dark brown hair. Seated at his desk with his face buried in the file, he muttered, "Whitman, eh? How old is he, would you say?"

"I'd say about eighteen," replied Micelli. "He's got a lousy case of acne, I'll tell you that much."

"That's a shame," DiPrima remarked flatly, peeling his navy jacket off the back of his chair. DiPrima always seemed larger than he actually was, even standing next to Micelli, who was almost a foot taller. Sporting a crop of salt-and-pepper hair, DiPrima was barrel-chested and fit, for a man pushing sixty years old. Rolling up the sleeves of his pressed white shirt, he folded his arms and tapped his foot impatiently. He had a borough-wide reputation for being a crack detective, and his father-like approach to prisoners and suspects had resulted in his obtaining more than his share of confessions, exemplifying the old adage that you can get more flies with honey than with vinegar.

Ayala, twenty years his junior, closed the file and glanced over at his partner. "You thinking what I'm thinking, boss?"

DiPrima nodded.

Micelli, meanwhile, scratched the back of his neck and breathed out slowly. "So what," he inquired quizzically, "if you don't mind my asking, are you planning, Detective DiPrima?"

DiPrima smirked and walked past Officer Micelli, heading quickly down the hollow corridor that led out to the street. He was more eager than he'd been in weeks. The case of Alma Estrada had noteworthy similarities to that of the Edmonds case, and it was important to determine whether a sex fiend was now threatening the already high-crime-rate area. DiPrima stopped, only for a moment, and turned back to Ayala, who was now reaching for his badge and cigarettes.

"What the hell, boys!" he hollered in a thick Brooklyn accent. "Are we gonna go talk to Whitman or Whitmore, or whatever the hell his name is?"

Close to the intersection of Pitkin Avenue and Junius Street in Brooklyn was a railroad siding. Next to the siding was a building, which housed the Schoenberg Salt Company. Although a good many of the company employees were regulars who received a weekly salary, many others would "shape up" daily for the job of unloading salt from railroad cars. DiPrima, Ayala and Micelli stepped from the squad car and walked over to the salt factory, where they questioned the manager. They were told no one by the name of George Whitman or Whitmore was on the payroll. Then they checked the salt company records, but they failed to come up with the name "Whitman" or any similar name among the regular employees. While it became readily apparent that the records were very poorly kept, and the names of those transient individuals were not always accurately recorded, the fact remained that there appeared to be no connection between George Whitmore and the salt company. The three men returned to the squad car and went over the file again. Now they were suspicious.

Seated in the back, Micelli reached up front and pointed to the file. "I wrote down 'Schoenfeld's,'" he insisted, his long finger pointed toward the document Ayala was skimming.

DiPrima grabbed the document out of Ayala's hands and held it outside the window so that the midday light illuminated the text.

Ayala lit a cigarette and, dangling his arm out of the right passenger window of the car, blew two smoke rings.

"The kid's a liar," Ayala stated flatly.

"I don't know, Detective. I tell you, this kid wasn't the type. He wasn't all there, if you know what I mean, but sincere as all hell."

DiPrima passed the file back to Ayala. He turned the key in the ignition and the motor roared. He glanced at Micelli in the rearview mirror. He couldn't get over what a rookie Micelli was—married to the ideals of justice, the swift and honest catching of a killer and closing a case. DiPrima continued to rev the engine, remembering when he was like that, decades ago. *If only the system actually did work*, he often thought. *Things now . . . Well . . . they were different.* Working for the Brooklyn North Homicide Squad had taken its toll. The endless crime, the lack of support from city taxpayers, the poverty and swindling, and the brutality—there was no end in sight. The Minnie Edmonds case, which he'd been poring over, was getting to him. He wanted answers. He'd seen that woman all cut up and left for dead. And maybe she was just another cold case; but just once, he wanted to know who did it. Just once, he wanted that somebody to pay for what he did. And sometimes, on a day like the one he was having, he just wanted out of Brooklyn altogether. If he couldn't catch this killer, if he couldn't give the Edmonds family a little bit of closure, then what was the point of it all?

"You okay there, partner?" Ayala called, his scruffy face twisting toward DiPrima.

"I'm just thinking, that's all."

DiPrima switched the car into gear and peeled out of the parking lot.

"Where we headed?"

"Back to the station house. There might be something to this kid."

Shellie Whitmore, George's older brother, cradled George around his neck and shoulders with his right arm as they walked to the Schoenberg Salt Company. George, who was generally soft-spoken, presented his story proudly, giving an animated account of how he told the officer that the suspect said, "Help me, help me. The law is after me," and how he illustrated for the officer where the suspect had escaped. Shellie listened intently to George, every so often rolling his eyes as if to indicate disbelief. Sensing George was winding down, Shellie stopped, turned to his brother and gripped his shoulder with his hand.

"Now you listen to me. You shouldn't be talking to no po-lice. And what you thinking, tellin' his white ass whose runnin' from johnny law?"

George hung his head, clearly frustrated. Shellie pushed George away with his hand and then poked him, hard, in the chest.

"And what you go on and tell that cop that you got yourself a job at Schoenberg's? You ain't got no job there."

George stumbled backward and struggled to regain his footing. His brother began walking, at a brisk pace, toward the entrance of the factory. And although George could barely see him in the near distance, as without glasses George could barely see anything, he still called out defiantly, "*Today* I'll have a job at the factory, Shellie. I will *today*, and that's the truth."

George Whitmore Jr. did not, in fact, gain employment at the salt factory on that day. Having forgotten to bring his Social Security card, a prerequisite for work at the company, George was denied employment. To redeem himself, he visited his girlfriend, Beverly Payne. Greeting her at the door, he concocted a dramatic story of how he went down to the station house and looked through photos of mug shots, trying to identify the assailant. George spent the majority of the afternoon at Beverly's, leaving late, long after the sun drifted behind the buildings and darkness fell, thick and heavy, over Brooklyn.

CHAPTER 3

Two days later

Before he was picked up by Detective Louie Ayala and Officer Tommy Micelli, George Whitmore Jr. had a bounce to his step. He had woken at dawn and wandered into the chilly April air, heading north along Amboy Street to Sutter Avenue. He turned west along Sutter Avenue, toward the Laundromat. And, as unaccustomed to the law as he was, particularly in Brownsville, George Whitmore Jr. was just naïve enough to believe that when Detective Ayala and Officer Micelli asked him to accompany them to the station house, he was simply being taken in to identify a real assailant.

The Seventy-third Precinct station house was a nondescript brick building on the corner of Bristol Street and New York Avenue. Whitmore climbed the cement steps with Detective Ayala, on one side, and Officer Tommy Micelli, on the other. He was excited to be privy to an unsolved case and eagerly climbed to reach the top of the stairs, where he entered the precinct. He was dropped off in a room down the hall.

George began imagining wild stories of himself as a detective, scouring the streets of Brownsville in search of crooks and killers, revealing his badge to wide-eyed shop owners and tenants. George remained easily distracted for half an hour, until finally, at approximately 8:00 A.M., the door opened to the squad room, where he had been left. Detective Louie Ayala walked in.

The detective had taken his jacket off and rolled up the sleeves of his heavily starched, clean white shirt. Detective Ayala had the arms of a prizefighter, and he often rolled his sleeves up to intimidate his suspects. That morning he was clean-shaven and smelled of soap and cigarettes. He glanced in Whitmore's direction, but failed to make eye contact. Then he motioned for him to get up.

"Sir—" Whitmore started, pushing his chair back in and following Ayala out of the room. In the doorway Ayala stopped so abruptly that Whitmore, who stood a few inches away, barely missed bumping into him. Then, with a long, hard stare, Ayala pointed his finger at George and said, slowly and steadily, "You don't talk, unless you're told to talk. Got that, kid?"

Whitmore nodded. Ayala repeated this remark a second time, more loudly and firmly, while George nodded readily. Finally Ayala turned and the two walked out of the room.

Meanwhile, Alma Estrada was contacted at home, and Officer Micelli was sent to bring her to the Seventy-third Detective Squad room, situated inside the Seventy-third Precinct. Officer Micelli was taller than Mrs. Estrada, and her neck extended back as she strained to meet his eyes. It was now approximately eight-thirty in the morning.

"You see this peephole, here?" he asked, pointing to the small hole in the office door. "Well, on the other side of it, we've got a possible suspect—I mean, this might not be the guy at all, but, if I may, would you mind taking a look through this peephole to see if we might've caught our man?"

Alma Estrada widened her eyes and lifted her hands in the air, as if to say something imperative. She wasn't sure she could emotionally handle seeing her attacker, let alone being so close in proximity to him. She told this to Micelli in rushed, frantic syllables. She knew her hands were shaking visibly and was relieved when the officer suggested she sit down for a moment. As they talked, he placed some telephone books in front of the door for her so that she could stand on top of them and see through the peephole when she was ready. Alma sat down momentarily, adding that, in thinking things through, she simply wanted to get it over with. She rested on the edge of the chair, waiting, wringing her hands impatiently, until finally Officer Micelli helped her up onto the telephone books. Alma leaned in slowly, her hands resting on either side of the peephole, fingers splayed evenly against the wood of the door.

"Bring him in," Micelli hollered.

Alma leaned in more, her left eye peering in through the hole into the empty squad room next door. The squad room door opened and she watched as George Whitmore Jr. entered. He remained where he was and looked to the office door, in exactly the direction of where Alma stood, pressed against the other side. She immediately pulled back; in her trembling, the door, which was already unhinged, began to open a few inches. Alma turned around to Officer Micelli, who had reached his hand out to steady her. "I think that's him," she said quickly and repeatedly. "I think that's him."

Micelli asked her if she was sure Mr. Whitmore was, indeed, the man who had attacked her just the other night on Sutter Avenue, and that it was very important that she be sure.

Alma pressed her eyes closed for a moment before saying, "Well . . . could I hear him speak?"

Micelli called out the request to Ayala, who then directed Whitmore to say the threatening words uttered by the assailant. A moment later, George Whitmore Jr. spoke slowly and clearly.

Standing there, Alma Estrada truly felt as if she were experiencing the entire night all over again. That voice—that soft, uncannily similar voice.

"'Lady, I'm going to rape you,'" he said, as instructed. After a short pause and some whispering from Detective Ayala, Whitmore spoke again, gently, but clearly.

"'Lady, I'm going to kill you.'"

Alma stepped back, almost falling off the telephone books. Micelli grabbed her and pulled her over to the table, sitting her down in a chair. He called to Ayala and they both sat with her while she confirmed, wholeheartedly, that George Whitmore Jr. was her assailant.

Next door, locked in the squad room, George listened intently. He could hear her say, over and over again, "That's the man. That's the man." He swallowed hard. Perspiration dotted his brow and his gaze fell toward the door, where his accuser sat, on the other side, utterly convinced of his guilt.

George Whitmore Jr. knew immediately as Detective Ayala and Officer Micelli reentered the squad room that things had gone from bad to worse. Ayala, who was puffing on a cigarette, jerked a chair out from under the table and sat down across from him. George's eyelids fluttered, adjusting to the smoke. He sat up, like a student in a classroom on the first day of school.

"Sir—" he began.

"So let's say you threatened to rape her," Ayala declared calmly, speaking in a thick, rough voice.

"No," George answered excitedly. "No, sir. I did not. I *swear*. You're making a big mistake here. I've never seen that lady before."

Ayala looked up at Micelli, who was towering over George, and said calmly, "Well, it's not like we don't hear that a lot around here, Mr. Whitmore. Right, Patrolman?"

Micelli nodded, resting his hands on the back of George's chair. Whitmore turned around, peering nervously up at Micelli. He smiled at Micelli, the only officer he was vaguely familiar with, but Micelli barely creased his jaw in return. Instead, he walked around to face Whitmore, leaned in ever so slightly, placed his long, narrow hand on the table in front of him and said slowly and softly, "George—you've got to tell the truth now."

Micelli paused a moment, making certain he had Whitmore's full attention. George, whose hands began to tremble slightly, nodded his head and, clearing his throat, replied, "But I am. I *promise* I am, sir."

Micelli's eyes remained fixed on George's. He placed his hand on George's shoulder and squeezed it, as he did two days before when the sergeant drove up on Sutter Avenue.

"George," he repeated, "it's going to be a whole lot easier for you if you just tell us the truth. Right here, right now."

Whitmore was confused by Micelli's stance. Just the day before, the officer had been asking him about the assailant, not treating him like one. He felt his eyes water as he stared at Micelli. George swore that he could see a note of sadness and remorse in the officer's face.

"I just don't know what you want me to say, Officer," Whitmore strained to answer. "I didn't hurt that lady."

At about eight forty-five that morning, Detective Joe DiPrima arrived at the precinct and was quickly escorted into the squad room where Whitmore was still being pressed by Micelli and Ayala. Upon entering, DiPrima sent Micelli out for coffee and Italian rolls. During the next hour, behind closed doors, the two detectives managed to get a confession out of George Whitmore Jr. Out in the waiting area, rumors circulated that voices were raised and furniture was thrown. It was very possible that Mr. Whitmore was beaten.

When Micelli was permitted back into the room, he found George seemingly unhurt. Instead, he was hunched over in his seat, eyes damp and hands resting on his forehead. The detectives were now asking him about Chester Street, which was the street where Minnie Edmonds had been found dead only a week before. Chester Street was only a few blocks away from where

Alma Estrada had been attacked. Micelli knew Detectives DiPrima and Ayala had been placed in charge of the Edmonds case. Suffice it to say, they were under a great amount of pressure to secure and close out the case.

"The boys fight on Chester Street," Whitmore remarked tiredly.

"Do you have anything on your mind about Chester Street, other than the boys fighting?" Louie Ayala pressed, lighting another cigarette.

Micelli watched as Whitmore swung his neck back. He looked drained, and the officer wondered if the two detectives had somehow worked him over while he'd been away. Not that Ayala and DiPrima were known for that kind of thing, but he had heard stories about the Seventy-third Precinct.

"What do you want to know about Chester Street?" Whitmore paused. "Does this have anything to do with the woman that was murdered there?"

DiPrima started writing on a sheet of paper.

"You tell us, Georgie. What do *you* know about the woman on Chester Street?"

George pleaded. "I don't know anything, sir—*please*. I didn't touch that lady, either."

Detective Ayala grinned and loosened his shoulder muscles by doing a few neck rolls. Then he began again, slowly and steadily.

"Come on, George, tell me about the woman on Chester Street. We know you know something. So why don't you just tell us?"

George covered his hands over his eyes; Ayala let out a deep, long breath. Then, as if choosing his words carefully, Ayala said slowly and deliberately, "We know you did it, Georgie."

Whitmore opened his mouth and drew in a breath. Micelli saw him hesitate, peering at the two detectives. Ayala was rubbing the top of his sandy brown buzz-cut hair, and DiPrima, with his sleeves rolled up and five o'clock shadow, was absorbed in the notes he was taking. Whitmore could hear the faint scratch of DiPrima's pen as it moved along the page. He asked if he could talk to Beverly Payne, but the detectives ignored him. Whitmore then glanced at Officer Micelli, pleadingly, and Micelli's face hardened. He shifted his gaze and focused on Ayala's cigarette, hanging over the ashtray.

Whitmore was losing hope; his behavior began to indicate that he was moments from giving up. Yet, as innocuous as he might've been, Whitmore was no dummy. Ayala jerked his head up and Whitmore looked intently at him—almost through him, it would seem. His voice was clear and slow, and to his credit, it was defiant.

"I don't know what to say—*sir*."

A little after ten in the morning, John E. Currie, DiPrima's commander at Brooklyn North Homicide, was notified that there was a suspect being questioned in the Minnie Edmonds homicide. Currie arrived at the Seventy-third Precinct at half past the hour, accompanied by Detectives Vic Arena and Edward J. Bulger. Upon arriving, Currie was notified that George Whitmore Jr. had, "in so many words," confessed to the Minnie Edmonds case. Upon notification he left, leaving Arena and Bulger in charge. As it turned out, while Ayala and DiPrima had managed to get a roundabout confession of murder out of George Whitmore Jr., they seemed unable to get him to locate the murder weapon. At first, Whitmore denied having a weapon and began retracting his confession.

"Georgie," Ayala said smoothly, "the only chance you got of getting out of this room today is if you tell me what the hell kind of knife you used, and where the damn thing is."

"I don't believe you," George mumbled, gazing downward.

"You don't believe me?" Ayala leaned back in his chair, throwing his hands in the air. He looked to his fellow officers, grinning broadly.

"He doesn't believe me," Ayala remarked to DiPrima, who looked up from his notes and shrugged his shoulders.

"Do you believe me, DiPrima?"

"You're an officer of the law. Of course, I believe you," DiPrima answered, gazing at Whitmore.

Ayala then asked Micelli if he believed him; to which, he nodded pleasantly. Ayala then turned back to George, hardening his expression.

"So, George, come on. Quit the games. Where's the knife?"

Whitmore began sputtering responses, but he was cut off by Ayala.

"Come on Georgie, you can tell me. Tell me where the knife is."

The room grew silent again, but for the scribbling of DiPrima. Whitmore folded his hands over his eyes for a minute. He sniffled; his nose was runny from crying.

"Okay," he said finally. "Okay."

"Okay, what?" Ayala answered softly.

"Okay, I'll tell you whatever you want me to."

"You tell us the truth, George."

"And you'll let me go, right?"

"And we'll let you go."

George Whitmore Jr. went on to describe the weapon as a black-handled, all-metal knife with a picture of a panther on each side of the handle. Officer Micelli had such a knife in his locker, so he produced one and Whitmore said his knife was similar. But when pressed as to where it was, he repeatedly denied knowing. Instead, he told them he lost it.

While they actually all got in a squad car and drove to the stairs of a tenement building on 178 Amboy Street, where George had slept that night, as well as to his girlfriend Beverly Payne's house, no knife was ever discovered. The police were eventually convinced that Whitmore had left the knife in the Amboy Street stairway and someone had since taken it. While the argument over the knife continued to escalate, and accusations persisted in bombarding Whitmore, by afternoon the officers had decided that—knife or no knife—they would book George Whitmore Jr. in both the Alma Estrada attack and the Minnie Edmonds homicide.

When Whitmore again inquired as to whether he could leave, the room grew eerily silent. Finally Detective Joe DiPrima glanced up from his notes and halfheartedly managed to say, "Not yet, kid. But maybe soon."

CHAPTER 4

Detective Edward Bulger had arrived at the precinct that Friday to deliver salary checks. On the squad room table was a copy of a paperback book that had been found in Whitmore's jacket on that morning when he was initially searched. It was called *The Tall Dark Man* and was, ironically, a suspense novel based around a young girl who is involuntarily a witness to a murder. Detective Edward Bulger saw it and began skimming through the book. He leaned his back against the wall and rested the bottom of the book on a slight beer belly, which had formed in recent years. The result of old age, he reasoned. Bulger was a man who, at first glance, was very handsome, with a chiseled jaw and infectious smile. Upon further examination, however, his hair, which was dark and trimmed short on the sides and top, was beginning to gray around his ears and his eyebrows. His cheeks and nose were ruddy, and his forehead was lined. Bulger had been "on the job" for twenty-six years. He had been a detective for seven years, and before that a patrolman, both in uniform and then plainclothes, investigating a variety of vice violations focused primarily on gambling and prostitution. He prided himself on being a first-grade detective, the highest grade a detective can attain. And, like most other New Yorkers, he, too, was shocked when he read about the Wylie-Hoffert killings in the newspapers. And, as luck would have it, because of the magnitude of the case, Chief of Detectives Lawrence J. McKearney established a five-borough, citywide task force to search for the "Career Girls" murderer. In early October 1963, five weeks after the crime, he was told to report to the Twenty-third Detective Squad in Manhattan to begin an indefinite tour of duty as part of the team of men working on the double homicide. It had now been many months since he completed his special assignment with his brethren working out of the Twenty-third Precinct. Yet, with the case still unsolved, Bulger found it difficult, if not impossible, to erase it from his mind.

Rolling a toothpick around in his mouth, he glanced up and saw a fellow colleague, Detective Vic Arena. Bulger said, "This is a sissy book. It's written for eleven-year-old girls. What gives?"

Arena shrugged his shoulders and began examining the articles on the table, one of which was George Whitmore's wallet. In doing so, he came across a photo of a white girl sitting in a Pontiac convertible. He passed the image to Bulger.

"Whatcha got there?" Bulger asked, scanning the photograph.

The images that Bulger found himself studying were, in fact, a snapshot of two young women seated—one was a blonde, with shoulder-length, wavy hair, most prominently displayed in the foreground. She was seated in the backseat atop the open canvas convertible, where it folded at the passenger area nearest the car's trunk. A brunette, with the side of her face depicted, was seated in the front-passenger side of the car. Bulger immediately closed the book and walked over to the squad table, where he studied the images more intently under a lamp. He flipped the photo over and found a handwritten inscription, *To George From*

Louise. He turned back to the image itself and studied the blond woman closely, under the light. He was awestruck. Only six months ago, he had been pulled away from Brooklyn to join forces with the Twenty-third Precinct in upper Manhattan. He was one of a lucky few detectives out of Brooklyn who were grouped together with Manhattan detectives to help solve the famous case of Janice Wylie and Emily Hoffert. And yet, following three months of tireless investigation, Bulger was sent back to Brooklyn, against his wishes, with the case no closer to an arrest than it had been the day of the murders.

Now he stood outside the squad room where George Whitmore Jr. had just confessed to one homicide and one attempted rape; and here, in his hand, he held an image that he was utterly convinced was of Janice Wylie. *That* Janice Wylie. Bulger scrutinized the photo: her hair, her delicate features, her figure. *This was her. It really was*, he thought, working himself up. *It just had to be.*

He paced the linoleum repetitively, circling the area outside the squad room. The steady tap of his shoes echoed through the corridor. He could barely wait for the door to open. Beads of sweat doused his brow as he anxiously anticipated his confrontation with Whitmore. He fantasized that the fierce "urgency of now" would inexorably lead to yet another Whitmore confession that day resulting in closing out the most celebrated brutal double murder on the books in the entire city. He would then notify his superior officers that he'd solved the case and outperformed his fellow detectives assigned to the Twenty-third Detective Squad in Manhattan. And like most of Brooklyn law enforcement, Bulger was tired of being seen as second rate compared to Manhattan detectives, and the Wylie-Hoffert case cemented that kind of thinking more than ever before.

But I have to be sure, he thought. He looked back at the photograph. His weary eyes were fixed on the snapshot held inches from his face. *That's her,* he repeated in his head, over and over. *It has to be.*

When the door finally did open, fifteen minutes later, Edward Bulger managed to replace Louie Ayala and began an altogether new line of questioning that jostled everyone at the precinct—but not nearly as much as the already deeply troubled George Whitmore Jr.

If Detective Bulger was surprised by or interested in the small stature of George Whitmore, or his seemingly gentle demeanor, he failed to show it. In fact, he began his line of questioning without any introductions. He entered the room swiftly, sat down in the chair directly across from Whitmore, rolled up his white shirtsleeves, placed the photo of the two women in front of Whitmore and said emphatically, "George, *where* did you get this photograph?"

George sat up, craning his neck to see the tiny black-and-white photograph resting in the center of the table. By now, he was hesitant to say anything, so he studied Bulger warily before sitting back in his seat.

"Now don't do that, George," Bulger said, amused. "What's with the blank look?"

Whitmore's eyelids batted nervously.

Bulger shifted his tone. He smiled and his lips widened, revealing smoker's yellowed teeth. He began questioning again. This time he sweetened his voice. His words were delivered slowly, as if he were a hypnotist advising the patient to stare at a swinging pocket watch.

"Now I asked you a question here, George. Where I come from, we address the person who's speaking to us with a proper answer. So I'm going to ask you again. Where'd you get the photo, kid?" Bulger pointed his index finger on the center of the image. His fingerprint embedded itself on the blond woman's face. "Don't lie to me now."

George opened his mouth and looked over at DiPrima expectantly, but the detective remained unresponsive. Whitmore turned his attention back to Bulger, whose eyes were serious, unfriendly and heated. Whitmore shrugged his shoulders, fully aware that this reaction would further add fuel to the fire. Instead, Bulger maintained his toothy grin, leaning back in his chair, which creaked as he shifted his body. With his right hand, Bulger tapped a corner of the photograph on the table in front of him. It made a steady ticking noise, which began to unnerve Whitmore.

"Where'd you get the photo, Georgie? Come on now."

George began panting for air as the term "where" seemed to be repeated endlessly—now by both detectives, their voices eerily calm and steady.

"I got it at the dump—"

"What?"

"I got the picture in a garbage dump in Wildwood, New Jersey . . . where I was living."

"What dump? What are you talking about, Georgie?" Bulger answered mockingly. "I ask you a direct question, and you tell me you got it at the dump?"

"I got it at the dump, where my dad lives, and I wrote on the back."

"You wrote on the back?"

"Yes, I did."

Without missing a beat, Bulger then said, "Didn't Detective DiPrima warn you about lying to me?"

"I'm not lying," Whitmore pleaded. "I got it at the dump. I—"

"You what?"

"I—"

Bulger was holding the image in front of Whitmore. His index finger was pointed at the blonde in the photograph.

"This girl here? You found a photo of this girl here at the dump? Are you sure?"

Whitmore, so intimidated that he could hardly speak, continued to stutter until finally he managed to say, over the top of Bulger's repetitive questioning, "I wanted to—"

"You what?"

Whitmore raised his voice. "—impress my friends," he finished.

Bulger flicked the photo across the table to Whitmore, causing him to flinch.

"I don't know, Georgie. It don't add up. Come on, seriously. Where'd you get the photograph? Why would you carry a picture like this in your wallet?"

Whitmore blinked repeatedly.

"I told you, Officers. I got it at the dump. Louise Orr is a girl that I'm friends with, and that there's her phone number," he said, pointing at some scribble written on the back side of the image. He paused before adding, "Just call it and she'll tell you herself."

Detective Bulger ignored this remark and changed his line of questioning: "You didn't steal it, did you?" Bulger reached across and grabbed the image back, glancing at the writing. He tapped on the image again. "Because if you did, you could tell me, you know?"

"I know."

"So you're really sayin', you *don't* know this girl."

Bulger reminded Whitmore of how he was already in a hell of a lot of trouble. One more lie and it'd be over.

Whitmore sighed, throwing his arms up in the air. "But I'm telling you the truth, Officer—that there is my handwriting, and I don't know the girl in that photograph. And I didn't steal it. I just took it from the junkyard. Nobody wants anything in a junk-yard."

"But it wasn't yours," Bulger reasoned, "so, in effect, you sorta stole it."

"I—"

Bulger lit a cigarette, leaned back in his chair and placed his feet on the table, one shoe crossed over the other. He flicked his match out, tossing it on the floor, and took a long, deep drag.

"Okay, kid, I'll play your game," he said coolly, exhaling a cloud of smoke. "So, for argument's sake, let's just say you did get this photo from a junkyard in . . . Where'd you say you're from? Wildwood. Wildwood, New Jersey. Fine. And then you tried to pretend it was given to you by this girl here."

Bulger pointed to the blonde in the photograph again. "So you wrote, 'To George From Louise' on the back." He fixed his eyes on Whitmore. "And maybe you carried this thing around in your wallet, like some sort of souvenir."

Whitmore tried to interrupt, and tried to defend himself, but Bulger had the floor and he wasn't about to open it up. The detective swung his legs off the table and stood up. He began slowly pacing around the squad table, until he reached Whitmore. Without turning to address him, he flicked the ash of his ciga-rette in Whitmore's direction. Whitmore rubbed the gray parti-cles from his pants and peered upward. He was exhausted now. The clock on the wall indicated that it was now a quarter past three in the afternoon, almost eight hours since he'd first been brought in. He began to wonder how much longer this ques-tioning would take, and if he'd *ever* see the light of day again.

"You stole it. Right, kid?"

Whitmore closed his eyes, attempting to hold back tears, which were welling up. He didn't care anymore. Nothing he said seemed to make a difference. He hung his head and rested his right hand on his forehead.

"Just tell the truth now. That's all I'm asking."

Bulger continued pacing the brief perimeter of the room, while DiPrima folded his hands and gazed across the table at Whitmore. When George opened his eyes, he turned to DiPrima, resigned.

"I'll just tell you what you want to hear," he said, half asking, half pleading.

DiPrima gestured for Bulger to sit down. He held Whitmore's gaze and replied plainly, "You just tell us the truth, George. You tell us the truth, and everything will be okay."

"Can I go then?"

Whitmore turned to Bulger, who was now seated across from him. He watched him stub out his cigarette in a half-full ashtray on the table. Bulger grabbed another cigarette from his pack of Lucky Strikes and offered one to Whitmore. George took it and leaned in for a light. Bulger struck a match and Whitmore watched the tiny flame as it crossed the length of the table. He inhaled, lighting the cherry, and sat back in his chair. Whitmore let out a cough. He hadn't had a cigarette in months; and even then, he wasn't really a smoker. But he thought this might calm the detective down, so he inhaled again. He was also grateful that Bulger wasn't pacing anymore, and that for the moment, anyhow, the room was silent.

"Yes," Whitmore said finally, "I guess you could say I stole it from the junkyard."

Bulger slid his hand along the metal table. He leaned back in his chair and whispered something in DiPrima's ear.

"That's good, kid. That's good," he said finally before stepping out of the room.

Detective Louie Ayala then entered the room and cuffed George Whitmore Jr. He then led him down the hall for formal booking on the Estrada and Edmonds cases. Whitmore could hear the steady click of a typewriter, the even chime sounding off at the end of a line. From behind him, he heard the tap of foot-steps, along with dull voices mingling and the sound of rustling paper. He heard his name spoken, over and over in hushed tones. George wasn't sure if he was being beckoned or if it was all in his mind.

"All right, kid," a familiar voice said, tugging him down the hall, "we've got more work to do."

It was Detective DiPrima. Whitmore had just been finger-printed and was now being taken somewhere new. He uttered, "Yes, Officer" serenely, hauling his legs up a long staircase and into a new, smaller, "more private" room, as DiPrima put it.

He settled into a metal chair beside a small metal table and studied the graffiti etched into the vinyl tabletop. Some of it in-cluded elaborate renderings of a person's name, like Reggie, carved in a sort of spiked font with a star carved where the dot in the *i* was intended to appear. Judging from these tags, Whitmore began to wonder how many more hours he would be seated in this chair. The room smelled of stale cigarettes and bologna sandwiches. The walls were barren and painted a dull white. There were two fluorescent tube lights overhead, one of which flickered every few minutes. Whitmore breathed in easy; his handcuffed wrists drooped in his lap.

Detective Bulger entered the room, and the two men as-sumed their positions from before. Bulger lit a cigarette and blew it at Whitmore, while DiPrima offered George a congenial ex-pression, as if to say, *You'll be out of here in no time. Just cooperate.* Bulger's sleeves were still turned up, and he cupped his hand around his jaw. His right thumb poked into his unshaven cheek. He flicked his cigarette toward Whitmore, an ash dropping on the center of the table. Whitmore didn't look up and didn't make eye contact. Instead, he sat, head bent, waiting anxiously for the next round of questioning to begin.

"This nonsense about Louise Orr isn't playing out, George," DiPrima began in a calm, steady tone. "So what's the real story, kid?" He paused for effect. "What are you hiding?"

Whitmore closed his eyes.

"George," DiPrima added gently, "we called that number on the back of the photo and we reached a courthouse in Cape May. In fact, the person answered saying she was in Cape May Courthouse."

"Georgie," Bulger inserted, taking another drag on his cigarette, "come on, kid—what are you playing at? Let me ask you— couldn't you have gotten that photo off of Eighty-eighth Street?"

Whitmore lifted his head and began gazing at the ceiling. He appeared to be averting his eyes from the flickering light that dangled from a rectangular metal shade, held up by a loose wire.

Bulger continued his questioning. "Didn't you go into the building on East Eighty-eighth Street and inside apartment 3C, grab the picture?"

Without shifting his gaze, Whitmore mumbled, "When can I leave here?"

"When you answer all our questions, George," DiPrima replied quickly.

"I don't believe you."

DiPrima leaned back in his chair and it squeaked as his weight shifted. He folded his arms.

"George," he tried, "come on now. I know this has been a tough day, but it's almost over. This is the last line of questioning." He paused. "I promise."

"You *really* promise?" George asked desperately, finally meeting DiPrima's eyes. DiPrima held his gaze and, without blinking, answered, "George, you have my word."

"George," Bulger echoed, "George, let me ask you that question again."

Whitmore turned to Bulger and asked for a cigarette. Bulger

pulled one from his pack, lit it, and passed it across the table. Whitmore brought it to his lips and inhaled deeply.

"George—did you get this photo inside the apartment at Eighty-eighth Street in Manhattan?"

Whitmore pulled the cigarette from his mouth and blew the smoke directly at Bulger. The room grew eerily silent for a few seconds, the light above flickering erratically. The air was cloudy with smoke and the three men—Joe DiPrima, Edward Bulger and George Whitmore Jr.—sat motionless, hearing only the sound of their own breath. Then, after some time, he spoke.

"Yes, sir, I did."

CHAPTER 5

By four-thirty in the afternoon, George Whitmore Jr. had confessed to having taken the subway to the Port Authority Bus Terminal and then transferred to an uptown train. Having taken some time to get this confession on paper, Bulger pushed forward, anxious to begin his line of questioning into the murders of Janice Wylie and Emily Hoffert. He asked George if maybe he had hit one of the girls on the head with a soda bottle, when entering the apartment. As an accident, Bulger reassured George, because the girl had startled him when he thought no one was home. Wasn't that the case?

Whitmore waved his hands in the air and nodded his head back and forth.

"—Not because you wanted to hurt them George . . . ," Bulger suggested promptly.

"I didn't hit nobody with nothin'," Whitmore answered defiantly, slinking back in his seat, his eyes shifting back up to the ceiling. Whitmore remained in this state for quite some time as DiPrima and Bulger revisited the line of questioning in a variety of different ways.

"You didn't mean to hit anybody," DiPrima tried; and then maybe "You forgot you hit her," Bulger attempted weakly. Realizing that they'd backed George Whitmore Jr. into a corner, the two detectives decided to give him a break and left the room for a few minutes to regroup.

Whitmore, who by then seemed to understand why he was there, also appeared conflicted as to what to do. He looked down at his hands, wrists scratched from the handcuffs. He studied the dirt in his nails and spread his fingers out wide.

Whitmore saw the round doorknob turn, and his heart skipped a beat. Then he gazed up tiredly as DiPrima and Bulger reentered, along with two other gentlemen dressed in plainclothes. One man was introduced as Lieutenant Currie, commander of the Brooklyn North Homicide Squad, while the other was presented as Inspector William E. Coleman, the commander of the Thirteenth Detective District. DiPrima and Bulger took their usual seats across from Whitmore, and the two other men stood to the side, against the wall. Whitmore turned and grinned awkwardly at Lieutenant Currie and Inspector Coleman; they returned his greeting with similar, awkward smiles. Cigarettes were passed around, matches struck and the room became clouded with trailing smoke. A Lucky Strike was offered to Whitmore; once again he took it, accepting a light from Bulger, who advised him not to pay any attention to their new guests. Paper shuffled, chairs squeaked as bodies adjusted in their seats and the tubular light from above continued its erratic flickering. A moment later, Detective Bulger began speaking—this time in a casual, if pleasant, tone.

"Look, George—I just got off the phone with the girls and they say they're not mad at you."

Whitmore stared at Bulger blankly.

"You didn't mean to do it. Right, Georgie? Isn't that right?" he added eagerly.

"No, I didn't . . . ," Whitmore responded almost inaudibly.

He had reached his hands up to his eyes, and the sound of the handcuffs clinking together overpowered his voice.

"What was that, George? Come at me again?"

Whitmore swallowed and repeated his statement.

"You didn't what, George?"

DiPrima echoed Bulger's query, leaning his elbows on the table. And in that moment, it seemed everyone in the room—from the shadowed men towering in the corners to the two detectives at the table—was bent over, mouths agape, breath paused and movement frozen.

"I didn't mean to hurt those girls," Whitmore managed finally, his voice a broken, stumbling mumble.

His eyes welled up. He fixed his gaze on DiPrima and then on Bulger, his voice coming through now—a faint, exhausted mess of syllables:

"Now . . . eh . . . can I pleeaase . . ."

He inhaled quickly—so quickly it sounded like a gasp. His nose was runny and he rubbed a finger along his nostrils and blinked erratically, as if his whole being had been shaken up.

". . . go home?"

News of George Whitmore Jr.'s surprising and dramatic statement, "I didn't mean to hurt those girls," spread through the precinct like wildfire. And such startling testimony kept on coming. Shortly after 6:00 P.M., George Whitmore Jr. had confessed, wholly, to the attack of Alma Estrada, the murder of Minnie Edmonds, and the double homicide of Janice Wylie and Emily Hoffert. In the hours following his initial confession to Detective Edward Bulger, Manhattan detectives John Lynch and Andrew Dunleavy, of the Twenty-third Detective Squad, arrived at the Seventy-third, along with Assistant Chief Inspector Joseph Coyle. Both Lynch and Dunleavy, of the Twenty-third Precinct, were familiar with the facts and details of the Wylie-Hoffert case. Yet, the Brooklyn police brass and detectives denied them direct access to question George Whitmore. In fact, they were only permitted to write out a list of questions that they wanted Whitmore to answer. This growing antagonism between the Brooklyn and Manhattan detectives resulted in fetching Captain Frank Weldon, the Manhattan District detective commander who was in charge of the investigation from its inception, to act as a mediator between the opposing borough detectives.

By eleven in the evening, James J. Hosty, a Manhattan assistant district attorney (ADA), arrived at the Seventy-third Precinct. The Homicide Bureau of the Manhattan, New York County, District Attorney's Office (DAO) had a procedure for its ADAs to be "on call"—the twenty-four-hour night chart—should a defendant in a homicide wish to make a statement. The process entailed the homicide detective assigned to the case to notify the ADA who was on call. The homicide detective then arranged for the ADA to be taken by squad car to the precinct where the defendant was being questioned. A young ADA, only in the DAO for three years, James Hosty happened to be the attorney on the chart and on call. After arriving at the precinct in Brooklyn, Kings County, he was advised by the Brooklyn Homicide Bureau detectives about all that had transpired, with particular detail regarding George Whitmore Jr.'s confession to the Wylie-Hoffert murders. Following this, and stretching deep into the early-morning hours of Saturday, April 25, Hosty took a Q&A statement from George Whitmore Jr., in the presence of Detectives Bulger and DiPrima and the New York County DAO stenographer Dennis Sheehan. Once again, and to everyone's satisfaction, Whitmore described the bloody details of the night in question. George had now been under interrogation for well over seventeen hours, and it showed in his statements. At one point, when asked if he had any weapon on him during the night in question, he answered by saying, "Yes, I have it right there."

Here and there, detectives would leave Whitmore in the interrogation room and revisit his statements. Finally, at approximately four in the morning, ADA James Hosty called his boss, Al Herman, the head of the Manhattan DAO's Homicide Bureau, and reported the confession. He advised Herman that the consensus seemed clear that the blonde who appeared in the photo taken from Whitmore's wallet was indeed Janice Wylie. Upon hearing this, Herman ordered that George Whitmore Jr., who had already been arrested by the Brooklyn detectives in the Minnie Edmonds and Alma Estrada cases, be booked for the murders of Janice Wylie and Emily Hoffert.

Early that morning of April 25, 1964, the street out front of the Seventy-third Precinct was packed with various officers and detectives, reporters, photographers and curious neighbors. Chief of Detectives Lawrence J. McKearney stood amid the mass of law enforcement and media and spoke confidently and proudly. As flashbulbs went off and a hum of whispers spread over the precinct steps, voices called out questions, each one drowning out the other—referring to the Wylie-Hoffert confession. McKearney said deliberately and clearly, "Whitmore told us details that only the killer could know."

Later that morning, Whitmore was arraigned in Brooklyn's criminal division courthouse for the Minnie Edmonds murder and the Alma Estrada attempted rape. Whitmore pleaded not guilty and was denied bail. The presiding magistrate effusively praised the outstanding work done by Brooklyn detectives. As Whitmore was led away to the Brooklyn lock-up detention area adjacent to the courtroom, he turned to his court-appointed lawyer, Harold Lasky, and said, with a puzzled expression, "Gee, I hope that the Brooklyn cops aren't angry at me for lying to them about committing those crimes."

CHAPTER 6

Two months later—late June 1964

Manhattan ADA Melvin D. Glass sprinted along Park Avenue, dodging pedestrians and vendors through the heavy doors of Grand Central Station. He then rushed down a flight of stairs into the hot, reeking and crowded subway platform just as the downtown express coasted to a stop. Its headlights blinded the waiting straphangers as it emerged from the vast tunnel. He dabbed his sweaty brow with a cotton handkerchief from his jacket pocket while inching his way through the masses into the already packed subway train. Edged against a door that continued to swing open, making a *whapping* noise each time, he straightened his navy tie, studying his reflection in the glass window. If this train didn't get moving, he'd have hell to pay, he thought. Normally, he carpooled into Manhattan from his home in the borough of Queens, but his car was in the shop—the diagnosis was slippery brake pads. So here he was, just another grunt, packed in like a sardine on his way down to the criminal courts.

At Fourteenth Street, the car emptied slightly and Glass moved from the doorway toward the center. He was thinking of something his sister, Blanche, a psychologist, had said the day before. They were discussing the Wylie-Hoffert case, which the media, in its frenzied sensationalism, referred to as the "Career Girls Murders." It was still a popular talking piece in New York that summer; and given that his sister worked just a few blocks from where the murders had occurred, it had grown to become somewhat of a family fixation. Glass had a friend, Detective John Justy, of the Nineteenth Precinct Detective Squad, who had been assigned to the Wylie-Hoffert case as the NYPD liaison to the deceaseds' families. Justy familiarized himself with the investigative facts of the case. Through him, Mel managed to visualize the extreme violence involved and found himself, not unlike many others, haunted by the idea of it. But what troubled him now wasn't the crime itself but the crime scene. Just the night before, his sister had said very directly, "From what you're telling me, the killer was compulsively clean, and that's something right there." *That's something, all right,* Mel thought as the train pulled into the City Hall/Brooklyn Bridge Station. He exited the train and walked along the platform, pushing through the turnstile and racing up the stairs to the warm concrete of Centre Street. He jogged south, half a block, and entered the district attorney's office and quickly headed up to court.

On his way into the courtroom, he ran into his bureau chief, Jim Yeargin, a tall, athletic, gentle, light-skinned black man, who had served in the Homicide Bureau for many years with distinction before being designated to run the Felony Trial Bureau, where Glass was now assigned.

"Mel, I expect you to lead by example. You know what they say about those early birds. We've got to get in court before those 'black robers' grab their gavels and take the helm," he said with a mischievous grin.

"Carpool fell through—won't happen again," Glass answered, panting.

ADA Glass gripped the sweaty handle of his briefcase, breezed into the crowded courtroom, secured the prosecution table and was ready to represent the People, just as the judge tapped on the gavel and called for order.

"One meatball sandwich."

Mel glanced up from his desk to find Detective John Justy, his good friend, balancing a tray of food before him, replete with sodas. He pulled out a chair across from Mel's desk and eased into his seat, setting the food on the desk, along with an open pack of Lucky Strikes and some matches. Mel gathered his paperwork and set it aside.

"Where'd you go? Poughkeepsie?"

"Very funny. Uncle Tony's was packed today, Mel. It's summertime—Jesus, everybody's down there but us."

Mel could smell the aftershave Justy had obviously drenched himself in and arched back in his chair. Justy wore his usual white shirt, which contrasted smartly with his nifty executive-style vested suit. Justy loosened his paisley tie at his throat.

"Heard you were running a little late this morning, ADA Glass."

Mel waved his hand dismissively and grinned. "I don't know where you heard that rumor."

Justy took a bite of his pastrami sandwich and through steady chews added, "How's that wife of yours?"

"Pregnant." Mel took a plastic knife and cut his sandwich in half.

"When's she due?"

"End of the summer—thank God. Betty's doing well and little Elizabeth's excited, but unsure if she wants a baby brother or sister."

Justy chuckled. For the next few minutes, all was silent in ADA Glass's office, except for the sound of sandwiches being gulped down and the whir of a small fan that rested in the back corner. Eventually, while sipping their soft drinks, the two men began discussing the Wylie-Hoffert case.

Pensively and almost imperceptibly, Mel edged his chair in closer to his desk, sat up and leaned forward with his elbows resting on the arms of his chair. He said, "Listen . . . I'm curious about something, and . . . well—"

"Well, what?"

Justy rubbed the palms of his hands together and quickly tossed the crumpled trash left over from his sandwich into a nearby wastebasket.

Mel continued, "Maybe you have a logical explanation?"

Justy blinked, leaning back in his chair. "Shoot."

"Well, my sister—you know Blanche, right?"

"Sure, sure. Met her once, some time ago. She's in the head-analyzing business, isn't she?"

"Sort of, a psychologist. Well, not for nothing, but she works just a few blocks from East Eighty-eighth Street, and, well, she's kind of gotten spooked by the case."

Justy rolled his eyes and said, "Jesus, Mel, who hasn't, for Christ's sake?"

Mel ran his hand through his shortly cropped dark brown hair, trying to think how to phrase his next question. He opened his mouth, but no words came.

"Spit it out!" Justy exhorted, folding his arms at his chest. "You're the one on the clock right now."

"Yeah," Mel answered with a touch of hesitancy, tapping his index finger on the metal top of his desk. "Well . . ." He cocked his head to the right before continuing. "Blanche was going on about how the killer apparently cleaned himself off in the bathroom after the murders."

"So?"

Mel watched as the door across the hall swung open and a few ADAs stepped into the corridor, heading down toward the elevator bank. He heard voices approaching his office and watched as a group of suits and ties shuffled down the drab hallway. As the chatter drifted off, Mel jerked forward and managed to say, as if an afterthought, "Well, she didn't think Whitmore fit that pro-file."

Justy raised his eyebrows. He pressed his elbows onto the desktop, resting his knuckles under his chin. "Didn't think he fit the profile?"

Mel rubbed his index finger just below his lower lip. A rise of laughter echoed through the hall as three more prosecutors came barreling through. Justy got up and gently closed the door.

"She thought the killer was compulsively clean," Mel reported.

Justy gave Glass a sideways glance. "Oh, I see, and Whitmore, being from the ghetto, can't be compulsively clean?"

Mel craned his neck. "That's not what I meant."

"Well, what *did* you mean, Counselor?"

"You yourself said that Whitmore was dirty, sleeping in a hall-way and disheveled when he was initially brought in. And besides, from the description of him, what's this kid from Browns-ville doing on the Upper East Side?" Mel folded his hands. With his fingers locked together, he stretched his arms the length of his desk. He added reluctantly, "It's nothing, I'm sure."

Justy pulled the door back open, studying Mel carefully. A young DA brushed past, a pile of paper extended from both his hands. Justy reached for his pack of cigarettes, pulled one out and lit it. Gazing at a photo on Mel's desk—a family portrait of Mel, his wife, Betty, and their daughter, Elizabeth—Justy squared his shoulders and narrowed his eyes. He frankly said, "Christ, Mel, you're not going to stop, are ya?"

Mel gave Justy a knowing stare and simply waited.

Justy eventually groaned, folding his arms at his chest. He closed his eyes briefly and then said quietly, "Maybe you ought to talk to Max Wylie."

Mel blinked, genuinely surprised. "Mr. Wylie?"

Justy took a drag off his cigarette, and then held it between his thumb and index finger. His expression grew somber. "Yeah, Janice Wylie's father. Just talk to him. Let's leave it at that."

Mel was genuinely surprised at his friend's unexpected stance. While Detective Justy was often earnest when discussing matters involving cases, he was rarely at a loss for words. In fact, he and Mel spent countless lunch hours discussing various details of particularly interesting homicides, or sometimes cold cases. An uncomfortable silence fell over the room. Justy fixed his eyes on Mel while pressing out his cigarette in the metal ashtray at the far-right corner of Mel's desk. Gray smoke dwindled, curling vaguely to the ceiling. The two men stared at one another. Finally Mel rested the palm of his hand on his desktop and said, with as much conviction as he could muster, "Give me his number then, Detective."

It was an understatement to say that Mel thought that he might be in a little over his head. While he had been with the DA's office for just six years, he was still small potatoes. At that time the longevity of the ADAs in Manhattan was widespread. Most were career oriented. Only two new applicants were hired annually. The senior most competent ADAs left the DAO to become judges. The legendary DA Frank Hogan office alum permeated every level of the state's judiciary—from the criminal courts, where misdemeanors were tried and felony hearings were conducted, to the state supreme court felony trial parts, up to and including the court of appeals, the state's highest tribunal. When first hired and before learning the bar results, the procedure at the DAO provided that the newbies were criminal-law investigators (CLI). Once the CLI passed the bar and was deemed admitted to practice in New York State, he became a full-fledged ADA. In Mel's case he was first assigned to the junior training rigors of the Complaint and Indictment Bureaus, where he presented about a hundred cases a month to grand juries deciding whether or not to indict the accused for the garden-variety mayhem inflicted upon the innocent denizens of Gotham. After that, he was assigned to the criminal courts to handle primarily arraignments, the setting of bail where appropriate, misdemeanor trials and dispositions, felony hearings, matters involving parole violations and evidentiary hearings ranging from defendants' competency to stand trial to the myriad of legal motions tendered by the defense. It was a fertile minor-league training ground. By 1964, Mel had made it to the majors, and was investigating and prosecuting felonies. Still, it was a far cry from getting his feet wet in the so-called "Career Girls Murders."

Mel leaned forward and cupped his forehead in his hands. His sister's suggestion that George Whitmore Jr. didn't appear to fit the profile of the killer was haunting him more now than ever. Besides, he should've been overly concerned—Blanche worked a mere three blocks away from where the murders took place. He needed to be able to assure her, wholeheartedly, that her neighborhood was safe again—that the murderer was behind bars, that the nightmare that plagued that peaceful stretch on the Upper East Side was finally over. And he certainly didn't like Justy's odd manner on things, either—that was entirely uncharacteristic even if his detective squad was told to keep quiet on things. It certainly never stopped him before. With Justy now long gone, Mel sat up and reached across his metal desk for his phone. Lifting the receiver, he began dialing the number and then waited; until after four rings, someone picked up.

A female voice chirped, "Lennen and Newell Advertisers. How can I help you?"

With as much assurance as he could muster up, he replied, "ADA Glass, with the New York County DA's Office. I'd like to speak to Mr. Max Wylie."

"Of course, Mr.—"

"Glass. Melvin D. Glass, of the New York District Attorney's Office."

"Of course, Mr. Glass. One moment please. . . ."

A few seconds passed before a male voice came on the line.

"Max Wylie here. What can I do for you, sir?"

"Mel—call me Mel . . . ," he added nervously.

"Okay . . . Mel. Listen, I'm at the office, so I'm afraid my time is limited. . . ."

Mel hesitated, trying to sort out just how, exactly, he could get to the point. After all, it hadn't even been a year yet. For half a second, the unspeakable horror of Janice Wylie's murder flashed through his head. He shuddered at the thought of her last moments alive; and worse, he considered the sight Max Wylie must've glimpsed upon entering that bedroom. Mel stared at the ceiling, quickly ruminating over various ways to approach the subject.

Before he'd chosen his words, Mr. Wylie spoke. "I'm sorry—Mr. . . . what was your name again?"

"Mel . . . Mel Glass. I work for the district attorney's office. You see, I've been chatting with Detective John Justy about the case and have some questions, just for purposes of clarification."

"'Clarification,'" Max Wylie continued flatly, "I thought you gentlemen made your arrest. I was under the impression my part in all of this was over."

"Well—" Mel tried.

"Say, I like the use of the word 'clarification' because I think this case needs some."

Mel tilted his head, pressing the receiver against his ear. "What do you mean, sir?"

"Exactly what I said. For starters, I'm following everything that's written in the press. And while I understand that the police and DAs aren't responsible for everything written in the papers, some people in law enforcement are leaking things to the media. According to news reports, the police are speculating that the killer or killers may have placed a blue blanket on the girls with the speculative notion, according to the stories, that these monsters or monster may have thought about carrying the girls down the service stairway."

"Yes," Mel agreed, "I've read that that's a possibility."

"Well, that's my point, Mr. Glass, about 'clarification.'"

Mel scratched the back of his head. "I'm afraid I'm just not following you, sir."

Mel could hear Max Wylie heaving a great, angry sigh on the other end.

"What I *mean* to tell you, Mr. Glass, is that *I*, Max Wylie, placed the blue blanket on my daughter and Emily, and the reason I did this was because I didn't know police procedure, and, Lord knows, I didn't want my wife or Kate Olsen to see the god-awful, frightful condition they were in. You have reviewed the crime scene photos, have you not?"

Mel held the phone in his left hand with his elbow resting on the top of his desk. He leaned forward. He was stunned. In a case of this magnitude, how could any type of speculation that appeared to be legitimate go on uncorrected? It was simply beyond his comprehension, and he was sure Max Wylie was mistaken. And yet, how could he be? How could a father forget a moment as horrible as that one? Mel stood up and began pacing his office, dragging the base of the phone in his other hand.

"Mr. Wylie, forgive me, but you're saying that you placed the blue blanket on your daughter? That's correct, is it?"

Mr. Wylie's voice rose. "Are you people incapable of getting anything right? *Yes*, that's exactly what I'm saying. *I* placed the blue blanket on my dead daughter!"

Mel ran his index finger over his lips and set the base of the phone back down on his desktop. "My apologies, sir. I just needed to confirm your statement, that's all."

Mel took this investigative blunder seriously, but what he was about to hear next was a complete game changer. There was no mistaking the anger percolating in Max Wylie's voice. This was a man who was simply broken in half, Mel reasoned. Max was desperate to shut that door—in fact, he needed to shut that door in order to survive. Try as he might, Mel was incapable of understanding what Max Wylie was going through; what it might be like to lose a daughter at the hands of a homicidal psychopath, and what it also might be like to have the whole city watch you crumble. Yet Mel tried. He thought of his wife, Betty, and of his young daughter, Elizabeth, and of the unborn child his wife was carrying. He reached deep, attempting to envision some madman laying a hand on them. A jolt rushed through him.

"The second point I'd like to clear up, Mr. Glass, if you're still listening—"

"Oh, I'm listening, Mr. Wylie, believe me. . . ."

"Good. Because when Mr. Whitmore was being questioned in the early-morning hours on Saturday, I was shown the photograph of the two girls in the car . . ."

"Yes, go on—" Mel grabbed his notepad and, cradling the receiver between his chin and ear, began frantically scribbling down notes.

". . . and I told the police that the girl in the photo was not my daughter."

Mel froze, his mouth agape and eyes wide in disbelief. He swallowed, feeling a dry lump in his throat.

"Are you listening to me?"

Mr. Wylie's voice sounded hollow traveling through the phone wires. Mel flinched.

"Did you say that you told the police the girl in the photo was *not* your daughter?"

"Yes, you heard me right. I know my own daughter, and that sure as hell wasn't her."

The moment Mel Glass hung up the phone with Max Wylie, he dialed Detective Justy, who answered on the first ring.

"Talk to me."

"I just spoke to Max Wylie. Can you arrange for me to get Whitmore's statement to the Brooklyn detectives, his Q and A to Hosty, all the DD5s and police reports . . . the whole case file, including the autopsy protocols?"

Without a pause Detective Justy answered. "It's done. You'll have it all tomorrow," he promised.

Mel hung up the phone, bolted out of his chair and headed down the hall toward the elevator banks. He had a number of cases hanging over his head that day, but he found himself suddenly fixated on one case only—that of Janice Wylie and Emily Hoffert. As he waited for the elevator that led upstairs to the trial courtrooms, he glanced down at his hands, noticing they were shaking. The issue of the blue blanket was one thing, and Max Wylie confirmed that he did indeed cover his daughter upon entering the bedroom. But Mel was floored by Max Wylie's second bit of information. The simple notion that Max Wylie confidently stated that the photograph Detective Edward Bulger found on George Whitmore's person—the photograph of two girls sitting in the open Pontiac convertible, which had *To George From Louise* on the back—the very photograph that the Brooklyn cops had deemed was of Janice Wylie, and being in the possession of Whitmore led to his arrest, was *not* a photograph of his daughter—why, it was simply incomprehensible. Here was a case of Murphy's Law: when things went wrong, they literally turned nightmarish.

"But, Mr. Wylie," Mel had remarked on the phone, shaking his head in disbelief, "are you sure?"

"One hundred percent, Counselor."

CHAPTER 7

Mel Glass remained at work late, poring over all of the case file police reports given to him by Detective Justy. Although it was a Herculean task to digest the voluminous nature of these reports in a case of this magnitude and duration, Mel set out to read every police report, DD5s (supplemental detective investigative reports), and police laboratory reports, including the autopsy protocol of the deceased girls. To get a sense of what this entailed, an average case at that time would have a single UF61 (complaint report) and one or two DD5s. In contrast, the Wylie-Hoffert case had over one thousand DD5s, which reflected the thousands of man-hours put in by various detectives working on the case. Mel had a good picture in his mind of what the scene looked like on the night of August 28. In fact, he had made it his business to reexamine the official police department photographs, including pictures of the bodies and the "death room." Like so many others before him, he was haunted by the Wylie-Hoffert case, and he just couldn't seem to wrap his head around the killer's profile. While he read and re-read the Whitmore Q&A/alleged confession, it just didn't click. What troubled Mel the most was that everything in the Whitmore Q&A

was already recorded in the police reports. There had to be something more—something more tangible than just documents—that could connect the dots. Then . . . he had an idea.

Mel picked up the phone and dialed a number he had scribbled down on a scrap of paper, which rested on the corner of his desk. Balancing the receiver between his ear and shoulder, he snatched up his pen and notepad with his other hand.

The other line picked up.

"Hello? Dr. Morris?" Mel asked.

There was a slight pause, and then—

"That couldn't be ADA Mel Glass, could it? At this hour?"

Mel chuckled.

"I should pose the same question to you, Doctor."

"Mel, how are you?" Dr. Morris asked earnestly. "You still hold the record for volunteering to conduct more competency hearings at Bellevue than anyone else."

Mel grinned. He stood up from his chair and began pacing back and forth in his office, holding the base of the phone in one hand and cradling the receiver against his opposite shoulder and chin.

"Well, in truth, I learned a heck of a lot from you. And in a very real sense, I'm still involved in checking out competency, although somewhat, Doctor, in a different venue."

"I'm intrigued, Mel. What patient can help your investigation today?"

Mel fell back into his chair, setting the phone base on the desktop. He took in a gulp of air and then, crossing his fingers, said, "Whitmore, Dr. Morris. I believe you have a patient there named George Whitmore Jr."

Around 9:15 P.M., Mel looked up from the stacks of police reports and walked out into the desolate, gloomy hallway on the sixth floor of the Criminal Courts Building. At the south end of the hall, toward the elevator banks, he gazed through a grimy window to the desolate side streets abutting the building. An occasional siren blast interrupted the evening's isolation.

Mel rolled his neck back, closed his eyes and sighed heavily. Among other details, Morris had revealed that Whitmore had an IQ south of 70, borderline mentally retarded—and that, Mel reasoned, very well may have been the underlying indicator that enabled law enforcement to extract the alleged confessions. In his heart of hearts, he knew that this was a crucial moment. He could easily go back to his office, close the files and return them, fully intact, to Detective Justy without another word on the matter. And he considered that option. He thought of his wife, Betty, and his daughter, Liz, and the anticipation of his new child. He reasoned that it would be easier to step aside, particularly while he and Betty finished putting down roots. Mel thought about calling Betty and asking what he should do. At the last second, however, he decided against it. Maybe he did so because he already knew the answer to that question; maybe he knew, too, how great the consequences might be if he was wrong. By 9:30 P.M., he still hadn't eaten, and yet his next move was inexorable. Mel picked up the phone and dialed a number he had memorized from his first day on the job. He waited; and when the other line picked up, he took a deep breath before speaking.

"Mr. Hogan," he began, "I hate to call you so late at home. . . ."

It was humid and overcast, with thick cumulous clouds rising above the skyscrapers. Mel Glass drove over the Brooklyn Bridge into downtown Manhattan. He parked in a lot designated for ADAs, which was two blocks from the DAO. Then he walked over to the Criminal Courts Building, which housed the district attorney's office, the grand jury rooms, the criminal courts, the judges' chambers and the Manhattan House of Detention for Men, more commonly known as "the Tombs." Mel entered the DAO on the Leonard Street side and took the elevator straight up to the eighth floor. He walked purposefully down the narrow hallway with its forlorn, putrid green walls, directly to the DA's office.

DA Frank S. Hogan was a legendary public official. He was the chief law enforcement officer in New York City and was regarded—among law enforcement, the judiciary, lawyers generally and the public—as the finest prosecutor in the country. While New Yorkers had a tendency to question the integrity of government officials, most people, counterintuitively, who followed New York's crime stories knew that Hogan ran an apolitical meritocracy since becoming DA in 1941, succeeding his mentor, Thomas E. Dewey. In 1935, it was Dewey who was appointed special prosecutor by Governor Lehman to root out corruption in the New York City justice system. Hogan left his Wall Street law office to become one of Dewey's top aides. Hogan was a lifelong registered Democrat, but he always had Republican, Conservative and Liberal party endorsement for his entire tenure.

When Mel reached the desk of Ida Delaney, the attractive young secretary who worked for District Attorney Frank S. Hogan, he nodded hello and Ida smiled in return. She wore a canary yellow minidress with a high collar, and her thick brown hair fell around her shoulders. Mel was already regarded as an up-and-comer, and he had friendly relationships with the office staff. After exchanging pleasantries, Ida picked up the office intercom and spoke softly.

"Mr. Hogan, Mel Glass is here. Okay, I'll show him in."

Ida then stood up and opened Frank Hogan's office door. She held out her hand to wave Mel Glass in. He passed her, stepping into the legendary office of one of his greatest heroes. He heard the door close behind him and peered forward toward the impressive wooden desk in front of him and the celebrated man behind it.

Frank Hogan was sixty-two years old in the summer of 1964, and his age was showing. His hair had receded at the forehead and was white as snow. Slight in physical stature, Mr. Hogan compensated for his lack of height with his bold and fiercely honest personality. During his early years with Dewey, he investigated and prosecuted many noteworthy cases of political corruption, organized crime and racketeering, gaining a reputation evincing unwavering honesty in the face of adversity. Nicknamed "Mr. Integrity," Hogan's fight to end corruption was boundless. He lived on 114th and Riverside Drive in a seven-room, river-view, rent-controlled apartment. He had no children. His true loves were—and no one ever really knew what ranked where—the district attorney's office, his office baseball team, known as "Hogan's Hooligans," Columbia University, where he attended college and law school and served on the board of trustees, and his wife, Mary.

DA Hogan glanced up from his desk as Mel Glass entered his office and motioned for him to take a seat. Mel felt his throat go dry as he edged his way over to Hogan's desk and sat down in a worn leather chair directly across from the man himself.

"Mel, I eagerly await your report," Hogan said, lighting his signature pipe with a box of matches resting on the edge of his desk. The aura of being in the presence of the legendary DA Frank Hogan and making a presentation to him created in the minds of his ADAs the notion that "you better be certain of what you say" and summon the best possible words to approach the subject.

"Come on," Hogan continued, "out with it."

To his core Mel was still the street-savvy kid who grew up in the hardscrabble, striving, working-poor and middle-class neighborhood in Brooklyn. He was schooled in the tough-as-nails competition of the school yard and excelled in the classroom. He was always the consummate team player, shunning the spotlight. His competitive spirit was tempered by a gentle and compassionate soul. His no-nonsense approach to doing justice was demonstrated early on when the indiscriminate bully met a lot more of his match after Mel chastened him for his social aggressiveness. Yet, Mel was not one to revel or gloat in victory. He always was just matter-of-fact.

Mel blinked, gathering his thoughts. He shifted in his chair and the leather squeaked slightly. He folded his hands in his lap; the Wylie-Hoffert documents were still resting neatly beneath them. Then he spoke slowly and clearly.

"Mr. Hogan . . . I certainly don't want to step on anyone's toes here. As you know, I'm not assigned to the Homicide Bureau."

Hogan nodded his head and waved his hand in a circular motion, indicating that he should continue.

"But I found myself intrigued by the Wylie-Hoffert case. Well, I did some research of my own, and I'm not entirely convinced that George Whitmore is the right man. In fact, I'm fairly certain he's not."

Hogan raised his eyebrows; his piercing blue eyes fixated on Mel, whom he regarded as one of his bright, idealistic acolytes. Hogan was, of course, aware of Mel's outstanding academic record, most relevantly highlighted by his University of Pennsylvania Law School achievement as managing editor of the *Law Review*. What most impressed Hogan, however, was Mel's integrity and mature judgment. He sought justice, *not* headlines. Hogan folded his hands, resting his elbows on his desk and hands under his chin.

"Well, then, please explain," the older man invited.

When Mel had finished briefing his boss, Hogan sat back in his chair, an upright leather desk chair with gold stud detailing on the sides. He imparted no sense of his mood to Mel, only his words, which came with a gentle smile and a quiet, if casual, tone to his voice.

"If you're right, Mel, that the Brooklyn police fed the answers to Whitmore in the questions he was asked that called for 'yes' or 'no' answers, how did they know so much about the case? Particularly the details of the location and manner of the killings?"

Mel then reminded Hogan about the five-borough, citywide NYPD task force set up a few weeks after the murders. The purpose was to gather detectives assigned throughout the city who investigated homicides and burglary/robbery cases to be briefed on the Wylie-Hoffert case in the event one of them came across a suspect who might fit the MO and, in fact, be the killer. Detective Edward Bulger, Mel explained, was not only assigned to the detective task force, but he stayed on for three months. Almost all the other detectives in the task force, Mel pointed out, stayed only about a week to ten days, just long enough to familiarize themselves with the facts. Bulger, on the other hand, appeared thoroughly engrossed—some would suggest even "obsessed" with solving the case.

Moments later, Hogan was on the intercom to Ida, asking that she bring around two of his men, Mel's bureau chief, Jim Yeargin, and Al Herman, who headed up Hogan's elite Homicide Bureau. For a few moments, sunlight streamed in through the open blinds, illuminating Hogan's desk, with all its various artifacts, case files, books and notebooks. Mel noticed a worn copy of *Moby Dick* resting on the very edge of the desk. There were a few pages clearly dog-eared; Mel couldn't help but wonder which pages they were.

Within minutes Ida escorted the two men into the office. Hogan motioned them to be seated.

Jim Yeargin was a six-three, lean, athletic and genial individual who had maintained his grace after serving many, many years successfully prosecuting scores and scores of murderers while assigned to the Homicide Bureau. His achievements were rewarded with his present assignment as head of the Felony Trial Bureau. Al Herman was a longtime, distinguished ADA, and one of the top trial lawyers in the DAO. As chief of the Homicide Bureau, he enjoyed one of the most prestigious positions in Hogan's office.

After Ida closed the door to his office, Frank Hogan addressed all three at once:

"Gentlemen—Mel came into my office this morning and told me something quite astonishing. Now I'm going to ask him to repeat what he said, and then I'll have a few comments."

Hogan turned to Mel and nodded.

Mel faced Jim Yeargin and Al Herman, both of whom had their arms folded at their chests. Yeargin smiled gently, while Herman appeared genuinely put-out, without even knowing what narrative Mel was about to convey.

"Well—I think there's a problem with the defendant whose been indicted in the Wylie-Hoffert case."

Herman furrowed his brow and held his arm out, as if cupping a baseball. In a deep, rough voice he then said, "What did you just say?"

Mel opened his mouth to speak, but Hogan held up his hand, motioning for Herman to hear Mel out. Herman turned and gave Hogan a quizzical look, but he dared not speak while his boss gave the order to listen. As was Mel's custom—with directness, logic and rational persuasiveness, he explained his doubts regarding the alleged guilt of George Whitmore Jr. In the course of a few minutes, Mel repeated all that he knew about the photograph found on George Whitmore. His major concern, he explained, was that in the Q&A, taken by ADA James Hosty, and in his alleged confession to the police, George Whitmore said that he found the photo in the apartment on East Eighty-eighth Street—and that it depicted Janice Wylie, the first girl he killed. But the wrinkle, or the A-bomb, was that Max Wylie remained emphatic that his daughter was *not* in that photo. If, indeed, that was the case, then George Whitmore's confession was totally untrustworthy and would not withstand the crucible of cross-examination, much less the standards of fairness that distinguished the Hogan office. Mel's second point, which had preoccupied him all night, was that after reading all the thousand-plus DD5s, autopsy protocols and the entire case file, he concluded that *everything* in the defendant's Q&A and alleged confession matched the police reports. Mel finished his presentation suggesting the real women in the photograph be found immediately.

Yeargin grinned approvingly, like a dad witnessing his son coming of age. He was always impressed with Mel's thoroughness and pure honesty, but this was a crowning achievement. If Mel's instincts and investigation were correct, and George Whitmore Jr. was innocent, then Mel would validate everything the Hogan office was all about—a true ministry of justice.

"Hold on just a minute," Hogan interrupted. "Mel, as I said to you before, you're suggesting that the Brooklyn cops unwittingly—in the most favorable light—fed George Whitmore all the answers during the interrogation because of the leading nature of the questions they propounded. Okay—assuming that to be the case—why does Whitmore go along with the program and confess?"

"Yes," Mel answered, nodding at Hogan. "I believe that's a real possibility, especially because they asked generally for 'yes' or 'no' answers. But there's another reason for my concern, which directly answers your question."

Mel paused, scanning both Yeargin and Herman, who appeared fully engaged in what he was saying. He was prepared to offer a rational explanation for Whitmore's irrational cooperation.

"Given the length of time Whitmore was interrogated," Mel continued, gesticulating with his right hand outstretched, "from about eight A.M. or so to four in the morning the next day, and the leading nature of the questions hammered at him, I decided to check with a doctor I happen to know at Bellevue, where

George Whitmore's been under scrutiny for the past couple of months. Turns out—"

Mel glanced over at Hogan, who appeared unaffected, but for a resolute expression on his face. He nodded again at Mel.

"George Whitmore has an IQ south of seventy, and the docs believe that he evinces a suggestive passivity when confronted with aggressive, intimidating authority figures. His father's abusive, violent and his older brother's got a sheet for violent crime. From what Bellevue tells me, cutting through all the psychoanalysis, is simply, given Whitmore's state of mind and violent home environment, he has a personality that wants to please, particularly when he perceives intense coercive circumstances."

Al Herman sat silent. He was visibly disturbed. As a seasoned veteran of the office, he understood the seriousness of the implications that arresting and indicting the wrong man would have on the office. It would undermine the credibility of law enforcement to a significant degree. He would have to take responsibility as head of the Homicide Bureau, if indeed George Whitmore Jr. was innocent. While listening to Mel's presentation, Herman was livid that he didn't have the Wylie-Hoffert case presented to the ADAs assigned to his bureau before presentation to the grand jury for indictment. After all, it was standard procedure. All homicide cases were routinely presented to the entire Homicide Bureau membership of ADAs, with, most notably, the senior members questioning every detail of the case to ensure that not only the defendant was guilty, but that all the evidence was obtained and the potential defenses were addressed and defeated. It was a special training lesson for the ADA who presented the case because he knew that if he wasn't thoroughly prepared, he would be chewed up by the bureau's senior trial lawyers. Amongst the most senior members were Vince Dermody, Bill Loguen and John Keenan. All three were regarded as not only the best prosecutors at the DAO, but also the finest trial lawyers in the city. And yet, because of the enormous caseload and the "so-called" confessions George Whitmore Jr. had made regarding the attempted rape of Alma Estrada and the Minnie Edmonds homicide, ADA Herman figured why waste the time on the Wylie-Hoffert case as well. That deviation in bureau policy, which was a staple of office procedure, would rankle Herman and cause grievous harm and damage to the credibility of law enforcement and potentially to the DAO's reputation.

Mel finished up by describing, in a bit more depth, Whitmore's passivity as described to him by Dr. Morris at Bellevue Hospital. Hogan, meanwhile, studied the demeanor of his two most trusted colleagues. Both were easy to read. For Frank Hogan the eventuality that Mel Glass was right was both a blessing and a curse. He waited for Mel to wrap up and then addressed all three.

"Gentlemen, as I see it, we've got three serious problems now. First, we don't go around indicting the wrong person. That's not what we do here." He paused for effect, adding, "Are you with me?"

Mel nodded swiftly, noticing Yeargin and Herman both answered "yes" in a kind of unified stupor. Hogan leaned forward in his seat, placing his elbows on his desk and folding his hands. He turned from Yeargin to Herman, looking each squarely in the eyes.

"Now, if we did arrest the wrong person, well, that means the killer is out there doing God knows what. And third—"

Hogan fixed his gaze, expressing displeasure, on Al Herman.

"Al—you're in charge of the office's elite core of trial lawyers, the best prosecutors in the business, and I'm wondering if and when the next shoe will drop!"

Herman stared at the floor and shook his head in self-disgust. Both Herman and Yeargin were Hogan's knights of the Round Table. These were men who had proven their mettle in the courtroom prosecuting vicious and depraved killers. They were not inclined to whine or blame others for their mistakes. Instead, they handled their responsibility with honor.

"Mel," Hogan said, simply concluding the meeting, "stay on the case, work out your existing caseload with Jim and report to Al and me what you learn."

Then he raised his finger in the air and added firmly and with gusto, "I'm particularly interested in that photograph, as I'm sure you can understand. I want to know everything, *everything*, there is to know about it."

CHAPTER 8

July 1964

It was another hot and muggy day in the city, even at nine in the morning. The air was thick and wet, and perspiration dripped from the skin of every New Yorker. In Battery Park, city dwellers found little respite in the slight breeze coming off the Hudson River, while in midtown pedestrians moved slowly, fanning themselves with folded copies of the *Post* or the *Daily News*. Downtown on Centre Street, Mel Glass was too distracted to notice the stifling heat. He took a sip from his coffee cup and studied a pile of paperwork on his desk as he leaned back in his chair.

Detective John Justy stood in the doorway of Glass's office. He was beaming. "I hear you picked up a new case, Counselor."

Mel nodded. "Yeah, yeah," he answered as casually as he could. "Come on in—sit down."

He tried to hold back the wide grin, which was forming along the corners of his face. He waved Justy in; then he folded his hands neatly on the metal lip of his desk. Justy pulled back the desk chair from the corner of Mel's office and sat down.

"I have some thoughts on how we should proceed."

Justy crossed his legs and tapped the end of a cigarette on Mel's desk. "I'm listening—"

"Well," Mel began, "the Brooklyn detectives believe the girl in the photo is Janice Wylie."

"I got that much, Mel," Justy inserted with a sigh.

"Hold on, John—now let's take a look at Detective Bulger."

"Okay, let's. . . ."

Mel looked intently at Justy. "Bulger comes in because it's payday on Friday, right?"

"Right," Justy answered, trying to evaluate where Mel's line of thinking was going.

"So he hears about Whitmore confessing. He's standing there in the station house with the checks. And then you've got these two Brooklyn cases a week apart—the Minnie Edmonds murder and the Alma Estrada attempted rape—in close proximity, and the Edmonds case is a stabbing. So there are already two cases that need to be solved, and solved fast."

Justy shifted in his chair. "Honestly, Mel, do you really think Detective Bulger just made it up for an arrest? That's one hell of an accusation."

"No, not exactly," Mel answered, treading carefully, "but I am saying that Bulger bet a lot on that image. I mean, he studies a photo that's found on the suspect and becomes utterly convinced it's that of Janice Wylie—*the* Janice Wylie, of East Eighty-eighth Street."

"Crazier things have happened," Justy reminded Mel, stretching his legs out in front of him.

Mel stood up and walked over to the door of his office. He scanned the dingy hallway and then loosened his brown-striped tie. "Right, but we also now know that Janice Wylie's mother, Janice Wylie's father"—Mel stepped back over to his desk, hovered behind it and leaned over, his palms pressed on various court documents, which were splayed on top—"and Janice

Wylie's friends all say that the girl in the photo *isn't* Janice Wylie." His eyes were wide and focused.

Justy stood and walked over for a better look at the court documents, then nodded perceptively. "So Bulger's wrong," he stated, closing his eyes momentarily.

Mel waved his left index finger in the air. "Not necessarily," he disclosed, with a mischievous grin, "but it seems the best way to confirm who is actually in that photo is to find out *where* it was taken, and at the very least, find *one* of the girls in the photograph."

Justy parted his lips and was about to counter Mel, when he noticed that Mel was gazing past him at something else.

"What? What is it?" he asked, swinging his arms out.

"ADA Glass?" a steady voice called out from the doorway.

Justy twisted his neck and glanced behind him. A black woman in a white dress and hat stood in the doorway, staring at Mel with a look of mild irritation. Mel knew immediately it had to be her—she looked like Whitmore. Brown skin, gentle but tired eyes, black hair with bangs curled down and a sleeveless white dress with ruffles at the nape of her neck. In fact, on closer inspection, he couldn't get over how much she and her son resembled one another—only she seemed weary from years of hard living. She was a thin woman, with a small frame. She looked like she was in her late thirties. Her eyes were puffy, as if she hadn't slept in years. She appeared cross to Mel, as if she'd been provoked her whole life and was just waiting for the next insult. He offered his most reassuring grin.

"You must be Mrs. Whitmore."

"Bernadine, please," she answered, stepping through the archway. She gave Justy a malign glance and then added, "You asked to speak with me here in your office."

"Yes, Mrs. Whitmore, thank you. Please have a seat."

She sat at the far end of the rectangular table protruding from

Mel's desk. Her back was to the wall, with Justy and Mel seated beside her on either side of the table.

"Mrs. Whitmore, I am Assistant District Attorney Mel Glass and seated across from me is Detective John Justy. I asked you to come here today because I need to find the truth about your son's case. I want to tell you right now that anything you say here will not be used against him in any way. Also I want to advise you that you do not have to answer any of my questions—you can leave at any time."

Bernadine tilted her head, fixing her hard, tired brown eyes on him. "You say, Mr. Glass, that you're searching for truth, but I haven't seen a whole lot of truth come out of these here courts, so excuse me if I don't exactly believe that you're looking for the same *truth* I am."

Mel blinked and fixed his eyes on Mrs. Whitmore. "Mrs. Whitmore, I know this is a horrible situation for you, and I know this is probably the last place you'd like to be right now, but you could be very helpful if you answered a few questions for me."

He paused for a moment and then added, "But it's entirely up to you. You can walk out right now and not tell me anything."

Bernadine Whitmore could feel her hands trembling and wondered if ADA Glass and Detective Justy could sense her weakness. She swore she wouldn't let them see her cry—she swore she wouldn't let them break her. And yet, as she gazed at Mel Glass, she couldn't help but think he might be on her side. She couldn't put her finger on it, but something in his eyes told her he was a God-fearing person who, just maybe, meant what he said. There was something about his expression—something in the way he sat, perched tall and thoughtful in his chair—that seemed to embody integrity.

"He didn't hurt no white girls."

Her voice began to crumble as she reached into her pocketbook for a handkerchief. Mel grabbed one from inside his jacket and quickly offered it to her. She extended her hand, looked intensely into his eyes and nodded approvingly when she accepted his offer.

"Mrs. Whitmore, please," he tried, "I just need to ask you a simple question."

She immediately stiffened and pulled herself together. She shifted in her chair and glanced over at Detective Justy and then back at Mel. Then she opened her mouth and her voice came steadily.

"My son may be slow, but he's *not* stupid. He has an excellent memory when he puts his mind to it, and he's quite a capable artist." She straightened her spine against the back of the chair and swallowed. "If I put my faith in you, Mr. Glass, what's to stop you from thinking me a naïve woman, who will be abused by the law just like my son?"

Mel nodded, but he said nothing.

"My George ain't ever been in Manhattan before, so why anybody thinking he done all these terrible things? Why?"

Her eyes welled up with tears, but she willed herself to hold them back.

"Mrs. Whitmore, I understand you're upset, I really do, and for good cause. If you put your trust in me, I promise that I will never deceive you. More than anything I'm only interested in finding the truth."

She watched Mel's eyes soften. He reached for the file that was situated in front of him on his desk. He opened it and pulled out the photograph of the blonde sitting atop the Pontiac convertible. Mel flipped it over and scanned the handwriting on the back: *To George From Louise*. Then he handed it to Mrs. Whitmore.

"Please tell me, Mrs. Whitmore, do you know where your son found this photo?"

Mrs. Whitmore glanced up warily. After a moment she accepted the photograph. First she held the side with the hand-writing on it up close to her eyes and then she flipped it over, studying the girl in the image. She handed it back to Mel after a few moments and again looked directly into his eyes.

They stared at each other a few seconds more and then Mrs. Whitmore nodded her head. She sniffled, blew her nose with a handkerchief from her purse and then managed to say wearily, "When I first visited my son in jail, I asked him where he found the photograph because the newspapers were making a big deal of it. The police in Brooklyn keep saying he stole it from the girls' apartment, the ones they say he killed. So I kept saying to him, 'Just tell me the truth. Where did you find the photo-graph?' My son is a good boy. He would never hurt anyone. He said, 'Mama, don't be mad at me. I know you told me so many times not to go to that garbage dump at home and pick through all that trash. But that's just what I did, and I found the picture there.'

"Oh, Mr. Glass"—she looked at him sorrowfully—"I did tell him plenty of times not to go to that garbage dump in Wild-wood. I figured if he found something valuable, it probably be-longed to some white folks and they would claim he probably stole it. But George just loved going there—I imagine for the adventure of what he might find. But he wouldn't lie to me—that's where he found it."

Mrs. Whitmore took a deep breath and then continued.

"This girl Louise, whose name appears on the back side of the photo, is a girl from Wildwood, and my George dated her a summer ago. She's a sweet girl, Mr. Glass, so don't go stirrin' up any trouble with her. Lord knows, she ain't done nothin'."

Mel nodded his head in earnest appreciation. "Thank you, Mrs. Whitmore. Thank you very much. You have helped me a great deal, and hold me to my promise to you."

He leaned forward and added with resolution, "I will find the truth."

Mel stood and extended his hand, which Mrs. Whitmore greeted with hers. Mrs. Whitmore stood up then and slipped her dress gloves back on her delicate fingers. Mel pushed his chair back; it let out a loud screech. Detective Justy walked over to escort her out the door. She gripped her pocketbook with both hands, as if her whole life were stuffed in its contents. She turned and glanced out into the busy hallway, where various members of law enforcement rushed back and forth. Then she jerked her head back around and gazed at Mel. She smiled, a trace of satisfaction; and then, taking a step back toward the archway of his door, she said, "Well, Mr. Glass, you sure got your work cut out for you, 'cause a whole lot of folks mistakenly think my son killed those two girls."

She paused in his doorway for a second and then added, nodding at him perceptively, "You know what I mean, don't you?"

He held her steely gaze and gave a gentle nod. "Mrs. Whitmore, I assure you that this office will find the truth, regardless of what others may believe about your son." Mel watched her as she walked back down the corridor at a steady clip toward the sixth-floor elevator.

Mel shook his head and, not missing a beat, walked back over to his desk. Justy followed. Mel grabbed his magnifier and scanned the image of the two girls and the convertible.

"You know," he said, pulling the lens forward and backward over the photograph, "I think I ought to speak to an arborist."

"What?"

Mel waved Justy over and pointed to a blurred area at the right top of the image. "Those look like tall trees."

Justy scratched the back of his neck. "Yeah, so?"

Mel looked at Justy and set the photo and the magnifying glass down. "Well, maybe it's like Occam's razor."

Justy fell back into the chair across from Mel's desk. "In English, please?"

"If I show this to an arborist, we might be able to save everybody some time and narrow the search for these girls. After all, Mrs. Whitmore corroborates her son's insistence that he got the photo from the garbage dump in Wildwood."

"Wow, you're serious," he said, trying to keep Mel's pace, "but just because the photo was in Wildwood doesn't mean the girls in it are from there."

In a flash Mel packed up his files, grabbed his jacket and started to head down the hall. One of the elevator doors was already open as Mel and Justy neared the end of the hall. He quickened to a slight jog and Justy followed suit. Reaching his arm out, Mel caught the closing elevator door on the far right-hand side. He smiled apologetically to the already rushed crowd of law enforcement and citizens in the car and stepped in with Detective Justy. The doors closed and they descended downward to the street.

At ground level Mel searched his pockets for a subway token. Justy held the main door open for Glass and then asked, "Hey, where are you gonna get this arborist?"

Mel stepped out into the noisy downtown street. He glanced back at Justy and grinned. "You know the maxim Occam's razor," he stated once more.

"Mel, what the hell is an Occam's razor?"

Mel folded his jacket on his sleeve and held his briefcase tightly in the other hand.

"My, my . . . famed detective Justy, the maxim is attributed to William of Occam, an English scholastic philosopher who believed that assumptions introduced to explain something must not be multiplied beyond necessity. Simply, John, the simplest explanation in a complicated scenario is usually correct."

Justy looked truly amazed.

Mel paused and then acknowledged, "I'm going to take the train up to the Museum of Natural History. I happen to know the curator there, who might lead us in the right direction."

"Sounds like you're on a roll, Mr. *Law Review*. Who am I to contradict," said Justy doubtfully.

"Oh, come on," Mel countered, "what's the worst that could happen? I get another shot to see the T. rex, one of my favorite ancient creatures."

CHAPTER 9

Mel hurried along Central Park West to Seventy-ninth Street. He climbed the museum's front steps, where he passed the famed ten-foot-tall bronze equestrian statue of Theodore Roosevelt. At the top of the stairs, he entered the American Museum of Natural History, where outside its walls, engraved amid four giant pillars, were three words Mel knew by heart: "Truth," "Knowledge" and "Vision." He stood in the central corridor, where one of the famed dinosaur fossils stretched high into the vaulted ceiling. Tourists and school groups flocked together on benches and spoke in hushed tones; footsteps clicked and echoed. Mel found himself studying a colorful mosaic, one of many that filled the vast halls. Thinking that he might be waiting for a while, he scanned the room for something to read. Over in the far corner sat a wall of exhibit pamphlets, maps and guides. He joined the crowd that had swarmed there and grabbed a few documents. A moment later a young man in a white shirt, tie and black dress pants walked up to Mel.

"Mr. Glass?"

He couldn't have been more than eighteen, Mel estimated,

examining the rosy cheeks, clean-shaven face and slicked-back blond hair of the gentleman standing before him.

"How did you know?"

The kid answered in one long run-on sentence. "People never know where to go here, and I'm always being sent out into the main corridor to recover various individuals scheduled to meet with Dr. St. Helme, and if you don't mind my saying so, you look like a lawyer."

Mel stood up and straightened his tie. "I do, do I?"

"Yes, sir."

"And you are?" Mel inquired with a friendly smirk.

"Peter," he answered brightly, leading Mel down a long hallway, through a narrow door and up a tight, winding side staircase to a very modest landing with three closed doors on the walls facing Mel. The floorboards were wide planks of old dark mahogany that creaked with each step Mel took. A few old red velvet upholstered chairs with brass nail-head trim rested between a long glass coffee table stacked with tattered issues of *National Geographic* and *Life Magazine*. Peter motioned for Mel to take a seat.

"Shouldn't be too long at all, Mr. Glass," he said, pivoting and disappearing back down the winding marble staircase. Mel wondered where the kid was headed next and then grabbed from his jacket pocket one of the pamphlets he'd snatched. It was all about the "Star of India," one of the largest gems in the world. Mel recalled it had been stolen from the museum just a few months after the Wylie-Hoffert murders. The story went that thieves unlocked a bathroom window during "open hours." Then they climbed in at night and managed to seize a number of gems, including the coveted 563-carat, grayish-blue stone, dubbed the "Star of India," valued at around half a million dollars. While the cat burglar, Jack Murphy, was caught a few days later, the famed jewel wasn't recovered until a few months later, far away in Miami, Florida, in a locker at the local bus station. Mel grinned at the thought of the thief trying to hide a jewel so big; he was amazed that it managed to escape all the way to the tropics of South Florida. He fanned himself with the pamphlet while glancing at another document advertising a North American Rare Birds exhibit, boasting 160 species. *No, thank you,* he thought, although he immediately felt guilty remembering a promise to take his wife out to see the World's Fair in Flushing Meadows. Somehow he felt as if she had mentioned a bird exhibition at the fair—or perhaps this was it. He flipped the glossy paper over and saw the image of a woman smiling pleasantly back at him. Her face was angular, pretty, with kind eyes. She wore her hair pulled back in a bun. Below the image, in fine print, was a name and identification—*Dr. Lucille St. Helme, Ph.D., Yale, 1940, Physical Anthropology.* Mel lifted the document closer, examining her cheekbones.

"Are you going to attend my rare-bird exhibit?" came a voice from nearby.

Somewhat startled, Mel jerked his head up and around. Dr. Lucille St. Helme, just as lovely as her photograph, peeked her head from around the corner. Mel stood up.

"How long were you standing there, Miss—"

"St. Helme. Dr. St. Helme." Her voice was light and airy, and she wore no makeup except for a dab of red lipstick. She stepped forward with her hand out. Her three-inch beige heels clicked and creaked on the floor below. She wore a gray skirt and a matching blazer, with a pair of thick black-rimmed glasses. She had dark hair pulled back tightly in a bun, just like in the photograph.

"Mr. Glass, is it? And you are *the* assistant district attorney?"

Mel smiled, and his cheeks flushed. "Well, that's what my mother tells all her friends, but, in fact, I'm just one of about two hundred others."

He reached out and shook her hand. She had small, thin hands, and her glasses drifted to the bridge of her nose. She laughed and then suggested Mel come into her office. He eagerly followed, stuffing the pamphlets back in his jacket pocket, and entered what was a relatively small but astoundingly spacious office. The floors still creaked, but the walls were white and the ceilings high, perhaps fourteen feet. There were windows on two sides— tall, old windows, with thick moldings. Along the north wall, Dr. St. Helme had a long wooden table piled with various artifacts, models, documents and books. Behind her desk was a wall of books stretching almost to the ceiling. Least impressive was her desk, which was bulky and worn, not unlike Mel's metal office desk. He admired the globe on the right side and found himself, standing there, spinning the metal orb absently. His index finger landed near Bangkok.

"Please have a seat, and just ignore the mess," she said. "I'm afraid I'm just back from South America. In fact, I have been doing a fair bit of bird-watching, Mr. Glass."

"Mel, please."

She motioned toward a forlorn wooden chair beside her desk.

"And call me Lucille. I'm sorry I can't offer you a better chair, but we spend our money on other things. . . ."

Mel didn't even look at the chair . . . he just fell onto it.

Lucille folded her hands and rested them neatly on her desktop. She smiled gently. "Well," she said slowly, "it isn't often that we have members of the district attorney's office up here, so I'm intrigued. I also have heard rumors that you're directly involved in the Wylie-Hoffert case."

Mel opened his mouth to speak, but Lucille cut him off.

"I don't live far from East Eighty-eighth Street."

She stretched her left arm out, resting her palm on a stack of magazines, and sighed. "I just feel awful about those murders— the person who committed those crimes acted like a savage."

Mel nodded. "Yes, it's an extremely tragic case, which is why I'm here. I'm hopeful that you can help me achieve some clarity with an important piece of evidence, Dr. St. Helme."

"Lucille," she corrected him gently.

"Lucille," he continued, reaching into his jacket pocket for the photograph in question and holding it out in front of her, "I need to find the location of where this photo was taken, which would be the starting point to find the two girls depicted in it."

They stared at each other knowingly. Silence fell over the room. After a few seconds, Mel dropped the black-and-white image of the Pontiac convertible on Dr. St. Helme's desk. She snatched it up and held it closer for a look.

"Are you familiar with W. H. Auden, ADA Glass?"

"Of course," Mel answered, "the poet." He then gazed contemplatively and cupped his chin with his left hand. He said, "'A real book isn't one that we read, but one that reads us.'"

It wasn't every day that her visitors could recite poetry. She was impressed, and she smiled before adding, "He also said that 'history is, strictly speaking, the study of questions; the study of answers belongs to anthropology and sociology.'"

Mel shifted in his chair and pointed his right index finger toward the photograph. "What do you think? Can you help me? I need to know where that photograph was taken."

Dr. St. Helme reached into her desk drawer and fumbled around, searching for her magnifying glass. After a moment her hand emerged holding a modest, circular magnifier with a narrow, brown leather handle. She held the tool close to the image, pulling it toward and away from her eyes.

"I interned with a famed arborist during my studies at the university—I should be able to sort this mystery out for you."

Mel leaned forward anxiously; Dr. St. Helme sighed, her eyes laser focused as she examined the image.

"That's a pitch pine," she announced, pleased with her discovery, then looked up. She studied Mel for a moment with a look of satisfaction in her eyes.

He waited for her to say something else. When she simply sat there, gazing at him with an excited grin on her face, as if she'd discovered the theory of evolution, Mel said, "Forgive me, Lucille, but I'm a simple guy. I grew up in Brooklyn. What's a pitch pine?"

Dr. St. Helme stood up and walked over to the long table by one of her windows. She grabbed a book, leafed through it and then handed it over to Mel.

He stood up quickly, held the book in his hands and gazed down at the image before him. It was a photograph of a tree. Mel couldn't help but find it to be a funny-looking plant, with multiple trunks and branches that sprouted oddly. In some ways it looked like a kind of bonsai tree. Dr. St. Helme handed the photograph of the two girls seated in the Pontiac back to Mel.

"Pitch pines are native to North America. While you can find them in various locations, specifically Maine and even northern Georgia, they thrive best in acidic sandy uplands or swampy lowlands."

She leaned against the table behind her, lifted an arm and straightened her glasses.

"It's the same type of tree, all right," Mel agreed, "but where do you suggest I start looking?"

Dr. St. Helme tilted her head casually and smiled. "Well, can you tell me about any location unique to this photograph that might be helpful?"

Mel responded, "When the defendant was first asked how he came into possession of the photograph, he said that he found it in a garbage dump in Wildwood, New Jersey. Subsequently I've learned from his mother that he told her that's where he found it. She also confirmed that, indeed, he frequently went to the garbage dump and scavenged around."

Dr. St. Helme grinned. "Very interesting. Given that the pitch pine is primarily located in a specific coastal plain, southern New Jersey, in and around the Shore, certainly qualifies as a legitimate site."

She turned and began sifting through a pile of rolled-up tubes of paper.

"It's here somewhere," she said absentmindedly. Mel walked over and stood beside her. He couldn't help but notice a lovely scent of jasmine and freesia. He glanced at her wrist. She wore a delicate Hamilton watch, with a thin white-gold roped band. The sound of paper, rolling and unrolling, echoed throughout the room.

"Here it is," she said eagerly, unrolling a wide, long document that revealed a map of the state of New Jersey. Mel leaned in. He could hear the sound of a pigeon cooing at her window. A taxi honked; wind from the fan beside her desk rustled the edges of pinned-down documents. Her finger slid along the delicate paper until it finally stopped at a small land area. The spot was covered with tiny illustrations of pine trees, positioned at the edge of the Atlantic Ocean.

"Here," she said, tapping her finger, "it's just between Philadelphia and Atlantic City."

Mel edged in closer, squinting, trying to get a closer look on the map. "Is it a town?"

Dr. St. Helme jerked her head up. "No, not really. It's very rural. Lots of lakes and campgrounds. The ground is acidic and sandy. You can practically drive through and reach the shore-line."

She continued speaking. "Mel—in the upper-right portion of the photo is what appears to be a body of water, most likely a lake. Yes, I think the Wildwood area is an excellent starting point for your adventure."

Mel glanced back at the photograph of the blonde in the Pontiac convertible and noticed the body of water that appeared through the trees. *Lake, campgrounds, sandy areas all around the pitch pines*, he ticked off silently.

"Well, I guess I have what I need," Mel said aloud.

"I guess you do," she answered.

There was an awkward silence before they both headed toward the door. Just as he was stepping into the hallway, she called him back. He turned. She was leaning in the archway of her door, a book held tightly to her chest.

"What is that other relevant Auden quote again?" She closed her eyes briefly. "Ah, now I remember. 'Murder is unique in that it abolishes the party it injures...'"

Mel smiled knowingly and continued, "'... so that society has to take the place of the victim and on his behalf demand atonement or grant forgiveness,'" he finished.

Her eyes beamed. "A pleasure, ADA Mel Glass, 'one of about two hundred,'" she said, extending her arm to shake his hand.

Mel accepted the gesture. With an affirmative nod, he smiled warmly and said, "Many, many heartfelt thanks, Dr. Lucille St. Helme, chief physical anthropologist, part-time expert arborist and full-time terrific individual. I can't tell you how much I appreciate your help. I owe you, big-time."

Belleplain State Forest lies to the north and the west of the city of Wildwood in Cape May County, New Jersey. It is a heavily wooded area, sprinkled with a number of lakes and campsites only a stone's throw from the pretty, bustling oceanfront communities of the Jersey Shore. Lake Nummy was the largest and most visited of the lakes in the region.

In May of 1956, on the day following the prom, the junior class of Wildwood High School held their annual picnic on the shores of the lake. At first, it appeared as though a downpour of rain might interfere with the planned activities, but, thankfully, as the morning progressed, there was a break in the clouds. The sky lightened, the rain let up and the elusive sun peeked out just before the picnic was under way.

Abbe Mills held her hand up to her eyes to shield the sun and walked forward, toward the lake, which was stretched out wide and shimmered. She had blond hair, blue eyes and a freckled complexion accentuated by a tan, the result of hours spent at sea aboard her father's boat. It was cool that morning and she wore a bulky plaid jacket over her cotton navy blue dress. She paused and pushed her short hair behind her ears.

"Don't you just want to dive in," she said, turning back to her friend Jennifer. "I *wish* I'd brought my bathing suit."

Jennifer Holley, a young teen in a sleeveless yellow gingham dress, paired with a white cardigan, rushed toward her. A plane bisected the sky and a male voice hollered, "Abbe! Come on!"

The blonde turned and hopped eagerly back toward the car.

"Jennifer," she called back, "should we take some snapshots?"

"Oh yes! Definitely," the brunette said, rushing toward her excitedly.

Back at the car, Lenny Meyers, Abbe Mills's date for the prom, was leaned up against the hood of his dad's brand-new Pontiac convertible. Lenny was a senior, and he'd been accepted into the University of Pennsylvania. He would begin his college education in Philadelphia that fall. He stood with another kid named Ricky Getz, Jennifer's date. The four of them had arrived at Belleplain well in advance of the bus convoy. Jennifer ran up to the car, reached inside and grabbed a case from the backseat. She pulled the camera out and began directing everyone to stand by the car.

"I hate having my photo taken," Lenny grumbled, rolling his eyes at Ricky. He crunched out a cigarette he'd been smoking, walked over and wrapped his arm around Abbe. The camera clicked and Jennifer arranged everyone a few more times before Lenny walked up and snatched the camera from her hands.

"Come on," he said, grinning, pointing toward the car, "go get the hell in the shot."

Jennifer made a face and then ran up to the car, jumping in

the passenger seat up front. Ricky sat at the driver's seat and Abbe was perched atop in the back. Lenny began focusing the camera.

"Come on, sweetie, give me a smile," he said, shuffling toward the car with the viewfinder against his right eye.

"Pass me a cigarette before the teachers get here," Ricky called out, pushing the car door open and darting over to Lenny.

"Hey, you're ruining the shot!" Lenny called, although he knew Ricky didn't care.

"Just get a shot of the girls," he said, holding his hand out for a cigarette. Lenny passed him his pack of Lucky Strikes. The pitch pines rose up high over the lake and swayed with a cool gust of wind. It blew Abbe's hair back and she reached up to hold it in place. Ricky lit his cigarette and Jennifer turned, seeing a bus coming up the unpaved road.

Lenny crouched down to frame the two girls, but, really, all he cared about was Abbe. She looked so happy, he thought. He reached his head around and winked at her. Just as he did, she called back, "Oh, Lenny, come on! Take the picture!"

Click. Her lips were parted in response, in a broad smile. Her eyes were squinting from the sun, and a cluster of pitch pines and Lake Nummy framed the background.

Jennifer had the roll of film developed at Taylor's Photo Shop in Wildwood. One print was made of each picture. The image of Abbe, reproduced in black and white, on the back of the Pontiac, was placed in an album in the Holley household. It remained there for five years, until 1961, when Jennifer discarded it along with a lot of other refuse. Shortly thereafter, it found its way to the Wildwood City dump.

CHAPTER 10

Bernadine Whitmore had great aspirations for her boys; she certainly didn't want them stuck in a junkyard that made very little money. However, her husband wasn't the easiest man to get along with, and money was scarce. They fought often over the demands he made of his children, and this created an atmosphere of tension that was always present in the household. On one occasion, of which she chose not to remember, words turned to violence and she lost partial sight in one eye.

When her husband's uncontrolled rage endangered her children, Bernadine oftentimes left her house for a few weeks in order to seek refuge with her sister in the Brownsville section of Brooklyn. On such trips she would take her younger children, Gerald and Geraldine, and sometimes she even took her teenage son George. He was a quiet, shy, unassuming young man who had very few friends. He liked to be by himself; when he wasn't searching through the garbage dump, he was drawing pictures. He drew in spite of severe nearsightedness and filled notebooks with various portraits of his family and the scenic views of the seashore, where he lived. He collected photographs, too, ones that had been discarded at the local garbage dump. When he was lucky enough to find a snapshot or two at the dump, he would take it home and render a picture of it.

Like most of the garbage dumps in the coastal towns of southern New Jersey, the dump in Wildwood attracted hundreds of seagulls, which were content making a home in its stink and clutter. They sat perched, waiting, watching in anticipation of when the city garbage trucks would drive in and unload things to eat. George Whitmore worked his way through the mass of seabirds and trash almost on a daily basis. The Whitmores lived down the road from the city dump in the western part of Wildwood. They occupied a small run-down shack, which looked as though it was about to collapse.

In the off-season there were no tourists; the town literally shut down when the weather grew cold. From late October on, Wildwood was reduced to its ten thousand permanent residents, who struggled to make a living. In the Autumn of 1963, George Whitmore's trips to the garbage dump increased. It was cooler; the trash didn't reek as much; his summer job ended, leaving him with very little else to do. To George, a visit to the garbage dump was something to look forward to. He never knew what he might find or when he might unearth some trinket worth a lot of money, which had been discarded by mistake, or something that had been thrown out by wealthy folks with oceanfront homes.

One afternoon he found himself kicking his feet back on a pile of worn tires that had been discarded at the dump. In the crisp, breezy air, he imagined himself a famous artist who earned millions of dollars and lived in a giant house with servants. He sat there and thought of all that money, of being able to take care of his mother and father and all his siblings. He conjured up images of his father abandoning the junkyard and, instead, laughing it up with his friends at the Golden Dragon, a nearby bar.

And then he thought of Louise Orr, a girl from Mayville, a town inland about ten miles. She was a pretty teenager and his mother knew hers; so on an occasional Sunday, the two families would get together. George was shy in Louise's presence; and while he never really dated her, he thought of her often.

On that day, though, he was slightly more distracted by a handful of photographs he had unearthed in the mountains of trash. One was the picture of a blond girl sitting on the back of a car. It was the type of picture that a fellow would be proud to carry in his wallet. It was the type of picture that a fellow could boast about to his friends, especially if his friends lived far away and didn't know the girl. It was the type of picture that a girl would give her boyfriend after she penned a note of endearment on the back. And so, using the sharpest pencil he had, George Whitmore Jr. wrote on the back of the photograph: *To George From Louise.* He put the picture in his wallet.

Up on 104th Street, resting like a fortress in Spanish Harlem, sat the headquarters of the Twenty-third Precinct on the island of Manhattan in New York County. A mere three stories high, it was sandwiched between Lexington and Third Avenues. On the second floor, all the windows sat open, as if its insides were choking on the stifling warmth. A metal fan by the left-side window whirred and circulated hot air throughout the room, up-ending loose papers and forcing weighted ones to flap in the steady current. Detectives John Lynch and Marty Zinkand both had desks positioned by the window, each one facing out, with views of another brick building painted white, its fire escape stretching upward, six floors, in a zigzag pattern. It had now been almost a year since the two detectives first arrived at the crime scene at 57 East Eighty-eighth Street, apartment 3C, where Janice Wylie and Emily Hoffert had been brutally murdered. Detective Lynch was also the detective who had the unenviable job of presenting the photograph found in George Whitmore Jr.'s wallet to Max Wylie for confirmation that the individual seated atop the Pontiac convertible was, in fact, his daughter, Janice. And while Mr. Wylie had insisted vehemently that the blonde in the photo held absolutely no resemblance to his daughter, like everyone else, Lynch knew that Whitmore had been arrested and the case was—insofar as he was concerned—closed. Nevertheless, Lynch saw fit to inform District Commander Captain Frank Weldon, who made no further communication of that event.

Mel Glass arrived at the Twenty-third Precinct and was directed to the second-floor detective squad. He climbed the steps and walked confidently down the hall. In the distance, toward the window, he saw Detective Lynch standing over his metal desk, gathering piles of extraneous paperwork and tossing them into his attaché case. Mel sauntered over as Lynch was shuffling the pile, cornering the edges into a neat stack, and leaned against the side of the desk.

"Detective Lynch, good to see you," Mel said brightly.

A police siren blared from the street below and Lynch jerked his body around and widened his eyes.

"ADA Glass?" He paused, waving his hand at Detective Marty Zinkand, who glanced up from the adjacent desk.

"In the flesh," Mel replied.

Zinkand bolted up and rushed over to Lynch's desk. A typewriter nearby clicked heavily and the neighboring phone began ringing. Finally, on the seventh ring, Zinkand leaned over to the empty desk and grabbed it.

"I'll call you back," he said into the phone on the empty desk, slamming the receiver down and gazing back at Lynch, who was scratching the back of his head. Detective Lynch then pulled out the toothpick, which he'd been casually rolling around in his mouth for the last hour, and said, without any further hesitation, "You got here fast."

Mel grinned and quickly shook hands with the pair of detectives. Detective Zinkand plopped himself down in a chair beside Lynch's desk; Detective Lynch leaned against the wall by the window with his arms folded at his chest and his black work shoes crossed neatly.

"Are you gentlemen ready?" Mel asked eagerly. "Better have your toothbrushes packed and have filled the gas tank to the brim."

"Where in Jersey are we going again?" Lynch asked.

Without missing a beat, Mel replied, "Wildwood."

Zinkand jumped out of his chair, with his mouth agape. He threw his hands up incredulously. "Now?" he asked.

"Yes, *now*, Detective," Mel said with a heavy sigh.

"But is this really about the Wylie—"

"*Yes*, the Wylie-Hoffert case." Mel nodded.

"But I thought—" Zinkand added, and stepped over to his desk, where he snatched a thick manila folder, clutching it under his arm.

"You can forget what you thought," Mel answered dismissively, "I'll tell you on the drive down."

Detective Lynch reached inside his jacket for his cigarette pack. He held the pack out to Mel, who turned him down with a quick nod. Then he lifted the pack toward Detective Zinkand, who pulled a cigarette out and lit it with a lighter he had in his hand. Detective Lynch also lit his cigarette, took a deep and quick drag and then said, "Wait a second. This is a postindictment case. You must know we've got a tremendous caseload at the Two-Three. I just don't get it. Why take two detectives off their busy chart for this?"

Before he gave up more information, Mel eyed Lynch and Zinkand, trying to get a sense of just how helpful these two detectives were going to be in the long run. Having read and reread the case file and related court documents, he had a pretty good idea of just how aberrant most formalities had become among law enforcement where the Wylie-Hoffert case was concerned.

Mel took a deep breath and then said very coolly, "Well, for starters, the big boss spoke to the chief of detectives, whom I have been speaking to, so I think you gentlemen can assume that your work today will prove vital to finally resolving some serious issues in the case."

Lynch and Zinkand sat dazed for a moment. They exchanged curious looks and then their eyes fell back on Mel quizzically.

"But what's in Wildwood?" Zinkand said, looking uncertain. "That's a run-down town on the Jersey Shore. Don't tell me there's another murder connected to this Whitmore kid, is there?"

"Jesus, I hope not," Lynch added, widening his eyes. He turned from Mel to Zinkand warily and then said, "That would bring in a whole mob of Jersey detectives. Haven't we had enough guys digging around in this case?"

Mel shifted his legs and paced beside Lynch's desk.

"What the hell are we looking for, anyhow?" Zinkand piped in.

Mel placed his hands in his pants pockets and focused on the detectives. Then he held up the now-famous black-and-white photograph of a blonde atop a convertible. Mel pointed to the girl in the photo and said, "We have to find this girl, and we have to find her quick. Now I've got reason to believe that she lives, or *lived*, somewhere near or in Wildwood, New Jersey. Whitmore claimed initially to the Brooklyn PD that he found the photo in the Wildwood dump."

Detectives Lynch and Zinkand sat wide-eyed, dazed and speechless.

Lynch cleared his throat and jerked his head around, exchanging looks of bewilderment with Zinkand. Then he held up his left hand, as if a student raising his hand in class.

"Yes, Detective Lynch—" Mel joked in his pleasant voice.

"Mel, what are the chances of finding this girl? We don't even know where this picture was taken."

Mel scratched the back of his neck and sighed. He stole a look at the desk clock and then carefully managed to say, "For one thing, we're never gonna find her sitting in our offices, and secondly, for the last several weeks, I've been working with a terrific detective in Wildwood and we've been checking out various locations, and he's just let me know some really good news. He's hot on a tip and it might work out."

Both detectives nodded absently. Lynch stood up and edged over toward the door where Zinkand was standing.

"And then?" Lynch managed hesitantly.

"And then, my friends," Mel shot back, "we'll find the real killer."

They sailed through the Lincoln Tunnel with the windows down. They looped around the on-ramp and shifted into the left lane on the New Jersey Turnpike.

Zinkand glanced in the rearview mirror and saw Detective Lynch gazing blankly out the window. "Hey, Mel," Lynch called out, "I thought you were on vacation?"

Seated in the front with Zinkand, Mel half smiled. "What can I say, my friend, when my boss is so interested in a case and finds it necessary to direct the chief of detectives to assign you guys to me, we're stuck together for the duration."

Zinkand nodded respectfully. Mel glanced back at the photograph of the girls in the convertible. *Maybe she's gotten married and has crossed state lines*, he reasoned. *Changed her name and moved out of the country. Who knows?* The only thing Glass did know was that she existed once, on one sunny day, and now she existed on black-and-white photo paper, on a white Pontiac convertible, somewhere near a pitch pine and near a lake with a funny name: Nummy.

Zinkand lit a cigarette and glanced over at Mel. "You know, Mel, the chief of detectives called me this morning to say that we're assigned to work with you. I gotta say your boss carries a lot of weight. I mean, really, one phone call from you and here we are on our way to the Jersey Shore looking for a needle in a haystack."

Mel gazed at the smoke coming from a nearby rooftop factory. "Could be worse. We could be heading to downtown Newark."

"Yeah, but, Mel, seriously, this is even more difficult than trying to find a needle in a haystack, if I may be so direct and blunt."

"I like blunt, go ahead."

Zinkand cleared his throat. "Let's face it, we have no idea where this photo was taken. And even if we find the location, we have no idea where the people are."

Mel smiled. "Good questions, but, like I said, I've got a tip—not a big one, but a tip, nonetheless. I've already talked to the Wildwood PD and they're on the case."

Zinkand sighed, dumping the ashes from his cigarette out the window. Mel rested his right arm on the ledge of the car door.

"Your doubts are well taken, Marty, but I'm telling you this is worth a shot." Zinkand shifted into the left lane and nodded. As the car zipped down the highway, Mel continued to explain. "If Whitmore didn't take the photo from the apartment, and we have good reason to believe he didn't, then his entire Q and A is worthless. Which means, in all likelihood, he's not our guy on Wylie-Hoffert."

They'd combed the area twice, and the sun was almost setting. Zinkand weaved his car down an unpaved, yellow sandy road. Lake Nummy shimmered up in the distance. They were eleven miles outside Wildwood in an area known as the Belleplain State Forest. Through Dr. Lucille St. Helme, Mel had learned that the area was located in northern Cape May County and the lake had formerly been a cranberry bog. Up ahead they saw a New Jersey state trooper and another individual. Zinkand pulled up beside the squad car. He turned off the engine and they all stepped out onto the crunchy gravel. It was humid out and Mel waved off a swarm of gnats, which had rushed toward his face.

"Watch it out here, Mel," said Detective Zinkand. "They've got these ticks and I hear you can get a disease."

Mel smirked, unamused. He walked over to the state trooper, wiping the perspiration off his brow.

The state trooper reached over to shake Mel's hand.

"Hi, I'm Mel Glass."

"Roy Edison here," the state trooper replied. "Hear you're chasing after a girl."

Mel nodded, glancing at the second man, who was taller, dark-haired and in need of a shave. This was the man of interest. Detective David Snyder, of the Wildwood Police Department, sauntered up to the out-of-towners.

"Hello, Mel, good to see you again," Snyder said, holding his hand out. The men all shook hands, and Detective Snyder then reached his arm out, pointing toward the water. "Mel, having studied the copy of the photo you gave me a couple of weeks ago, and having combed the area pretty good, I'd say the water in the background of the photo is from this lake and the trees are definitely pitch pines."

Mel jerked his head around toward the lake, tapping his foot into the mossy ground.

"You mean, we're at the location?" he asked, astonished, exchanging glances with Detectives Lynch and Zinkand, who both already had their mouths parted and ready to speak.

"It sure looks like it to me," Snyder replied.

Trooper Edison remarked, "This girl also looks vaguely familiar."

"Yeah, I think I might know where this girl lives," Snyder added.

"Just so it's clear to us, you're referring, David, to the blonde in the photo?"

"That would be the one, Mel," Snyder confirmed.

Detective David Snyder led the way in his car with State Trooper Roy Edison. Mel, with Lynch and Zinkand, followed directly behind. They drove through the center of Wildwood, New Jersey, which reminded Mel a little bit of Coney Island. He could smell the cotton candy and caramel popcorn wafting from the concession stands. Mel glanced at a blinking theater marquee on his right—*Bikini Beach*, with Frankie Avalon and Annette Funicello. A street vendor selling Italian ices hollered out from behind his cart, "A nickel for an ice!" The salty scent of the coast filled the air and Mel could feel the anticipation and adrenaline coursing through his system as they turned a corner and drove into a residential area, where they finally pulled up to a modest two-story colonial, white with black shutters. Mel practically leapt from the passenger seat up front, slammed the door and darted over to Detective Snyder, who was calmly leading the way up the driveway to the front door.

Before they even rang the doorbell, a young woman appeared behind a screened-in door. It was hard to see beyond the metal screen, but Mel noted that she had blond hair—short—similar to the photograph. The woman inched the door open and said, in a slight but friendly voice, "Can I help you?"

Mel edged his way to the front and reached for the photograph once again. He held it up in plain view of the woman, whom he could barely make out through the screen.

"Yes, miss, I believe you can. We're looking for the woman in this photograph."

She opened the door and peered out a little bit. *Blue eyes, too,* Mel thought. The door creaked slightly.

"May I hold that?" she asked gently.

Mel nodded and offered it through the door. After a moment

she handed it back. Then she opened the door and stepped out onto the landing.

"Well, yes," she said curiously, "the girl in that photograph is me. It was taken about eight years ago or so, I guess."

The detectives exchanged looks of disbelief. Mel steadied himself, took a deep breath and then said, "And do you mind if I ask what your name is?"

She considered him warily. "Am I in trouble?" she plaintively inquired.

Mel grinned. "Not in the slightest."

"Well, in that case, my name is Abbe Mills Romano."

CHAPTER 11

October 1964

The midmorning traffic heading downtown on East Broadway was its usual frustrating gridlock. If you were in a hurry, in order to make any progress in a southbound direction, you had to operate your car like a football running back who runs to daylight by zigging and zagging and diving forward, wherever he sees daylight.

Detective Patrick "Paddy" Lappin picked and chose any vacant opening through which to maneuver his official NYPD vehicle. He bobbed in and out of the snarled traffic. As he weaved among the cars, he miraculously avoided contact with other motorists who were of similar minds. So, understandably, he wasn't paying much attention to the prisoner sitting in the backseat when the younger man spoke.

"Yo, Paddy," Nathan "Jimmy" Delaney said in a thick New York accent peppered with the hipster slang of the early 1960s. "You know, I think it was JFK who said, 'Life is unfair.'"

Lappin glanced up at the rearview mirror to see Delaney. The scruffy, thin man, who was handcuffed in the backseat of his unmarked squad car, was a well-known figure to the detectives in the Twenty-third Precinct. The thirty-five-year-old had been in and out of jails and prisons for most of his adult life, mostly on small-time drug charges. The veteran detective's hound dog–like face and doleful brown eyes hardly changed expression as he responded, "Yeah, him and a few others."

"Let's face it," Delaney continued with a sneer, "if I was some silk-stocking type, you're not my escort to the criminal courts. In fact, now that I think about it, I'd probably be living large in my pad at the Plaza, while my lawyer appeared before some judge to get my case dismissed. Can you dig it, my friend?"

Dead in the water in traffic, and now stopped by a red light, Lappin turned in the driver's seat and looked over his shoulder at Delaney. The cop shook his head. "Are you kidding me or what, Jimmy? You've got a sheet as long as my arm. You shoot heroin and sell that shit to whoever has the dough. You've done enough time in the can to get several graduate degrees, and you just stabbed to death one Roberto Cruz, albeit under arguably legit circumstances. And somebody's doin' you an injustice? Give me a break!"

"The hell, 'arguably'! Cruz, the lowlife, slugged me with a steel rod," Delaney complained. "What was I supposed to do? Ask him if he was agreeable to arbitration? You know damn well it was self-defense."

"Well, then, my friend, your lawyer better be able to convince the DA or you could be going away for a long time," Lappin replied as he searched for an opening through which to surge at a moment's opportunity.

"Hey, listen, Paddy, screw my lawyer!" Delaney exclaimed, leaning forward and speaking urgently. "I can't afford for this case to go the wrong way. It'd be just my luck to get some hotshot, snot-nosed young DA looking to make a name for himself. No, no lawyer . . . I got something special for the DA, which I plan on telling him myself."

"Oh yeah?" Lappin said dryly. He was used to prisoners who

claimed to have some "special knowledge" to get them out of trouble. "So what are you selling, Jimmy? Care to share your ace with me?"

"Why not? And I'll up you one," Delaney retorted. "You can tell the DA that you guys got the wrong cat for the 'Career Girls Murders,' and me and my old lady know who did it."

Lappin looked up again into the mirror and noted the desperation in his prisoner's eyes, but there was also something in his voice. Almost a cockiness. By the time they reached the Criminal Courts Building on Centre Street, that intuition that all good detectives possess was telling him that this wasn't something to ignore.

The Manhattan House of Detention for Men, the Tombs, is situated at the most northern end of the towering gray Criminal Courts Building complex. On the sixth, seventh and eighth floors of the opposite side of the edifice are the offices of the district attorney of New York County, which is comprised of the island of Manhattan. The middle part of the building houses the criminal courts, with the judges' chambers sitting on top of them.

After handing Delaney over to the corrections officers (COs) inside the Tombs, Lappin went in search of the detectives he knew were working on the Wylie-Hoffert case with the district attorney's office. Unable to locate the point man for the investigation, he returned to the Twenty-third Precinct, where he went looking for his squad commander, Lieutenant Thomas Cavanaugh, and told him about his brief conversation with Delaney.

As it turned out, Cavanaugh, a twenty-five-year NYPD veteran, eight of it as a detective squad commander, had his own doubts about the "Brooklyn Psycho," as some of the media had dubbed George Whitmore Jr.

"Hey, do me a favor, Paddy," he suggested. "Give Mel Glass a call. I think he and his wife just had a baby and he's taking some time off, but he's looking at the Wylie-Hoffert stuff. The scuttle-butt is that the Whitmore case is in trouble."

"Sure, I know Mel, too," Lappin replied. "Good guy. I've worked with him on some other cases, and he's real sharp."

Lappin walked over to his desk and looked through his file cards for the home telephone number of Mel Glass. He dialed the number and was rewarded when the young ADA picked up the phone.

"Mel? This is Paddy Lappin," the detective said.

"Hello, Paddy, to what do I owe the pleasure?"

"It's been a while, kiddo," Lappin said, "and I understand congratulations are in order."

"Yes, yes, thanks," Glass replied. "My son, Paul, was just born, and I've been staying home, taking care of my daughter, Liz. But I'm sure you didn't just call to congratulate me."

"Yeah, I hate to disturb you," Lappin said; then he paused for a moment before going on. "But I heard something regarding Wylie-Hoffert I thought might interest you."

"Go ahead, I'm all ears," Glass responded.

"Okay. It may not be much, but my gut tells me it's worth a look-see," Lappin said, adopting his official police-speak demeanor. "Here's what I got. A local dealer up here in the Two-Three named Nathan Delaney—though he goes by Jimmy—recently stabbed another low-life drug dealer to death. From everything I know about the case at this point, the deceased—one Roberto Cruz—hit Delaney on the head with a steel pipe, only to be dispatched by Delaney with a knife to the throat. Un-less I get some unforeseen evidence, it looks like a pretty solid case of self-defense. . . . Anyway, on the drive downtown to the Tombs, Delaney tells me we've got the wrong guy on Wylie-Hoffert, and he wants to speak to the DA in charge. So here we are."

"What do we know about Delaney?"

"Several convictions for drug sales and possession, and one attempted robbery. He's done his share of time. But he's no skel."

"What do you mean by that?"

"Delaney's not the usual drug addict off the streets," Lappin said. "He's a smart guy—went to City College and has a high IQ—he's also a marine veteran. I wouldn't bother you at home, but maybe he's got something of value . . . or maybe not."

"It's definitely worth a shot, Paddy," Mel replied. "I appreciate you getting in touch. Let's set up a meeting with Delaney ASAP in my office, and get me the file on the Delaney-Cruz case, if you would."

A few days later, Mel Glass waited patiently in his office for Lappin to arrive with Jimmy Delaney and his wife, Margie. He glanced at a recent photograph on his desk of his newly expanded family: his wife, Betty, his daughter, Liz, and his newborn son, Paul.

Mel had enjoyed the time he took off to spend with them, as well as putter about their small, cozy home in Queens. He'd particularly liked the family's evening walks in the neighborhood, with the leaves beginning to turn color as September moved on to October.

He and Betty had even taken the kids to the World's Fair, held at Flushing Meadows Corona Park in Queens. The fair's theme was "Peace Through Understanding" and was dedicated, according to its advertising, to "Man's Achievement on a Shrinking Globe in an Expanding Universe." It was a showcase of American technology and know-how epitomized by a twelve-story-high stainless-steel globe of the Earth called *Unisphere*.

Still, for all the distractions, Mel often found himself thinking about the Wylie-Hoffert case and making plans for when he returned to the office. In particular, he went over and over in his mind the afternoon they found Abbe Romano, who happened to be visiting at her parents' home from out of town.

* * *

Hesitantly, Abbe had invited him and the detectives into her parents' house, where she talked in detail about the day the photograph had been taken.

Abbe told Glass that she'd never owned a copy of the photographs taken that day at the after-prom picnic. Her friend, Jennifer, had only made one print of each and had placed them in a photo album.

Although he knew what the answer was going to be, Mel still asked her if she'd ever met Janice Wylie, Emily Hoffert or Katherine Olsen. Or could she think of anyone who might have lived in their apartment building on East Eighty-eighth Street? The young woman shook her head. She'd heard of the murders, of course, but didn't know the victims or anyone who'd lived on the fashionable Upper East Side.

As he got ready to leave, Mel thanked Abbe Romano and asked if she'd be willing to testify about what they'd just discussed. But the young woman's eyes had grown wide with fear and she shook her head vehemently. No, she was married now, to an attorney, and they lived in a small town. She didn't want anyone associating her with such an infamous murder case. Someone might think she was somehow involved with the killer, she worried, since he'd been carrying a photograph with her in it.

No assurances from Mel that any court appearance would be short—and the DAO would make sure the record was clear about her noninvolvement with the crimes or the killer—could convince the young woman to change her mind. He'd have to talk to her friend, Jennifer Holley, if he wanted someone to testify about the photograph. She'd given him an address for Holley and was only too relieved when they left.

Mel and his team were able to find Holley soon after. She'd repeated the story they'd heard from her blond friend, including that there was only one copy of the photograph. She was surprised to see it in the possession of the police. Her father had died in 1960 and her mother decided to sell the family home when Jennifer joined the Peace Corps in July 1961. Before she left, the young woman had gone through her things and had thrown a lot of it away, including the photograph taken at Lake Nummy. And, no, she'd never met the victims of the "Career Girls Murders" or anyone else who lived at that Manhattan apartment.

Although he'd suspected that the one piece of physical evidence linking George Whitmore Jr. to the crime scene—the one item that corroborated his confession and statement—wasn't trustworthy, the reality of what that meant was staggering. First, Detective Edward Bulger would have never even questioned Whitmore about the Wylie-Hoffert case without it. Second, it also meant that Whitmore told Bulger the truth the first time he was asked about where he got the photograph, and that he'd then been badgered into making a false confession. Without hesitation he'd told the Brooklyn cops that he picked up the photo in the dump in Wildwood, New Jersey. Third, Whitmore's faux confession was the fusion of his own psychological weakness and the relentless leading nature of the questioning process. If the George Whitmore Jr. statement in the Wylie-Hoffert case was untrustworthy, what was the value of the incriminating statements he made in the Brooklyn cases?

Yet, Whitmore had been indicted based on his confessions, the Q&A statement and the photograph. He was facing a double-murder charge in New York, and his trial for the Estrada case was coming up in November.

Mel's reflections were interrupted by a knock on the door. He looked up to see Detective Lappin standing there with a man and a woman, who he assumed were the Delaneys. He invited them to take a seat around the small conference table set up perpendicular to his desk in your basic armless Port Authority uncomfortable chairs. He quickly introduced himself and gave a brief history of his experience at the DAO and prior relationship with Detective Lappin, whom he described to the couple as "one sharp, perceptive and highly skilled" detective. "And he says you might have important information about the Wylie-Hoffert case."

Jimmy Delaney grinned and shot a glance at the detective. "I thought you might want to talk to me," he said, and then looked at Glass. "I can dig it, but I ain't giving this away. I might need it someday." He paused and then, as if unable to keep completely quiet about the information, added, "I will say that the cops already talked to the cat who did those girls."

"When?" Glass asked.

"Right after it all went down. When the cops were pulling everybody and their mothers in for questioning."

Glass looked at Delaney, who held his gaze rather than looking away, a sign that he might be telling the truth. "So you really believe your guy did it?"

The drug addict leaned forward as he looked Glass in the eyes. His breath smelled like he hadn't brushed in days and his sallow face had several days' growth of beard. But he spoke clearly and earnestly when he said, "I *know* he did it. He came to my pad about noon that day and said he was in trouble because he just killed two chicks during a burglary. He had blood on his pants and he wanted a change of clothes, and he wanted to shoot up."

Delaney then leaned back in the chair and crossed his arms. "Now that's all we're going to say, man," he added, nodding at his wife.

CHAPTER 12

"*Now that's all we're going to say, man.*"
When Delaney made his declaration, Mel had to think quickly about how to handle the confrontation. He knew the interchange between him and the Delaneys would go a long way in establishing a relationship that could be invaluable in uncovering the real killer.

Mel was aware that Delaney—who had been around the block a few hundred times—was trying to see how far he could push and outmaneuver a young ADA. Mel figured that if he came on too aggressively and cowed Delaney into giving vital information, there would always be that uncertainty that he might grow resentful and "flip," changing his story without warning. Yet, if Mel appeared appeasing and weak, Delaney would control the relationship and make demands that could ultimately evaporate his credibility as a potential witness. He would have to find just the right level to get to the truth and corroborate whatever the Delaneys might say.

So let the chess game begin, Mel mused before addressing the couple. "You're here because you told Detective Lappin that you and your wife know who murdered Janice Wylie and Emily Hoffert. It's up to you, Jimmy. You can leave this room anytime you want. As far as your case goes, you say you want immunity before you talk. But you know I wouldn't comment on any deal unless I know exactly what you've got to offer and how I can get it corroborated."

Mel paused to study Jimmy's face. The smirk remained on his lips but his eyes were serious. "I want the truth, pure and simple," Mel continued. "And if you're going to give it to me, we're going to have to trust each other, so let me tell you about the status of your case. I've learned from Detective Lappin that it appears to be a case of justifiable self-defense. Your case will be presented to the grand jury and, most likely, you'll walk. But that's as far as I'll go right now. . . . One word of caution . . . I'll know, believe me, if you're telling the truth or not."

Glass let that sink in and then moved his queen. "I want you to understand," he said sincerely, "I don't take you for some street skel junkie with a long sheet. That's not who you are, Jimmy. Some time ago you took an oath when you joined the Marine Corps to defend your country and its citizens against 'all enemies foreign and domestic.' It's all about service. I served two years in the army, and I know something about service, too. Now tell me the truth and you can be part of freeing an innocent kid sitting in a jail in Brooklyn and helping bring to justice a stone-cold killer. That's it. It's not too late for you to define who you really are. If you trust me, you talk. If not, you walk. It's your call."

Delaney's eyes met Glass's, but the smirk was gone. He and Margie sat silently in thought. Neither of them trusted the justice system—though, in truth, much of the blame lay with them. But Mel could tell that they were wondering if maybe he was for real. If not, they'd know soon enough. Grand juries generally did what the DA presenting the cases asked. If Glass was a liar, Jimmy might find himself facing a murder trial, where anything could happen.

Finally Jimmy Delaney broke the silence. "Mr. Glass, I'm a multiple offender, a two-time felony loser, but I acted in self-defense with Cruz, just as you would have under the same circumstances," he said. "It's true I've made a lot of bad decisions, and you're right, we need to trust each other. So let's get to it." He looked at his wife. "I know the drill. Margie, they're going to take you to another room so they can talk to us separately. I'm going to tell Mr. Glass everything, and you should, too, honey."

With that, all four people stood. The couple hugged each other and Margie was led away to an adjoining office. Jimmy watched her go and then sat down again. "His name is Robles. Richard Robles. He lives at 214 East Eighty-ninth Street with my wife's aunt, Dolly Ruiz."

For the next hour, Mel mostly listened as Delaney told him about the day Robles showed up at their apartment. "It was a little before noon on August twenty-eighth," Jimmy explained. "He said he was in trouble—that he'd just killed two girls during a burglary. He had blood on his shirt and his pants, and was wearing a jacket he said he got from their apartment and carrying a paper bag. He said he took a couple of cabs after leaving the girls' apartment to get to our pad. He needed a change of clothing and I gave him pants and a shirt. There was some money from the burglary that he gave me to buy drugs."

Delaney claimed to have left the apartment to buy the drugs, while Robles stayed behind with Margie. "I was gone about forty-five minutes," he added. "When I got back, he was still talking about it. He said one of the girls gave him a blow job."

After shooting up, Robles left the apartment, but he'd returned that night with newspapers that were already carrying the first stories about two young women who'd been stabbed to death on the Upper East Side. "He said those were the girls he killed," Delaney noted.

Robles had returned again the next day with more newspapers. "There were pictures of the girls in the paper, and I thought the blonde was real pretty. I asked him, 'Why'd you have to kill them?' And he said the blonde wasn't as attractive as the newspaper was making her out to be."

Robles also told him that he got in through a window. And that when he'd told the second girl to take off her glasses, "She said something like, 'No, I want to be able to identify you.' He got a couple of soda bottles and hit them on the head to knock them out. Then he started stabbing them. I remember him saying that the smell almost made him throw up. One of the girls died right away, but the other one wouldn't die and he had to stab her a few times in the heart. Then he went into the bathroom to wash up."

When Jimmy Delaney finished his story, Mel Glass got up and went into the next office, where Margie Delaney waited. She was a tiny woman with stringy, dark hair and was missing three of the fingers on her left hand. He knew from Jimmy that they had three children, ages seven to eleven.

After offering the woman a cup of coffee, Glass said, "Jimmy says you can back up his story. Is that true?"

Margie Delaney nodded and, cautiously at first, gave her account. The more she spoke, the more Mel was convinced that he was hearing at least some version of the truth.

Despite his growing excitement, Mel kept his cool while the Delaney woman continued her narrative. As soon as he could, without revealing the thoughts that were racing through his mind, Mel told Margie that he needed to take a break. Then, as nonchalantly as possible, he joined Detective Lappin and Lieutenant Cavanaugh in the hall outside of his office. The lieutenant had been informed about the possible breakthrough in the case.

"What do you think?" Cavanaugh asked.

Mel took a moment to gather his thoughts before answering. A rush to judgment had already resulted in the indictment of an

Janice Wylie and Emily Hoffert were slain in their apartment on Manhattan's Upper East Side on August 28, 1963. *(New York Daily News/Getty)*

The front of their building at 57 East 88th Street, looking west.

The entrance to the victims' residence.

The double doors leading into their building.

The lobby of 57 East 88th Street, showing the door that led to the service area. Access to this door became an important issue at the murder trial.

The bedroom where the murders took place. A knife—one of the murder weapons—is seen on the radiator (circled).

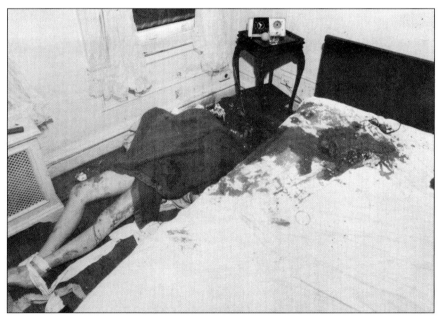

The victims, partially covered with a blue blanket placed on their bodies by Janice's father Max Wylie when he found them. The clock radio, unplugged by the killer, showed the time as 10:35. Emily's glasses are on the bed, and the handle of the knife is seen on the radiator.

The bathroom located near the bedroom where the bodies of Janice Wylie and Emily Hoffert were found. Note one of the murder weapons that the killer placed on the bathroom sink.

The living room, facing the windows. The TV was on to show Martin Luther King, Jr., delivering his historic "I Have a Dream" speech in Washington, D.C.

The living room, opposite view, facing the door to the apartment's hallway.

Interior view of the kitchen window in Apt. 3C. The killer entered the apartment through this window.

This exterior shot shows the kitchen window of Apt. 3C, as well as the window of the service stairway, through which the killer exited to climb into the apartment. The numbers indicate the floors of the building.

Exterior of the kitchen window of Apt. 3C. The handwritten notations were used in the courtroom to show the jury how the killer entered the apartment.

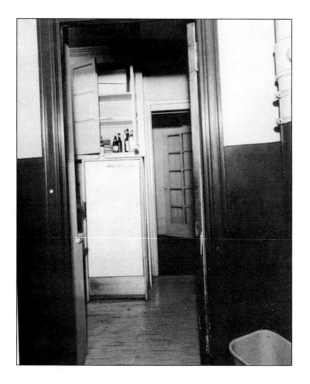

The kitchen, seen from the service stairs.

The service stairs and door to the apartment.

Entrance to the basement—the killer's access route into the building.

Interior of basement. The killer walked through this area to reach the service stairs.

The tunnel leading to
the west courtyard.

Rear courtyard of the
crime scene.

George Whitmore was taken into custody by Brooklyn Detectives Edward Bulger (left) and Joseph DiPrima (right) in April, 1964. *(New York Daily News/Getty)*

This photo, found in Whitmore's wallet, was used first to incriminate him, later to exonerate him.

On the back of the photo Whitmore wrote, "To George From Louise."

DA Frank Hogan was featured on the cover of *The New York Times Magazine*, July 23, 1967. *(Sam Falk/The New York Times/Redux)*

DA Frank Hogan at his desk. *(Sam Falk/The New York Times/Redux)*

Frank Hogan with executive assistant DA David S. Worgan and chief assistant DA
Alfred J. Scotti. *(Sam Falk/The New York Times/Redux)*

Mel Glass (right) with
colleagues ADA Frank
Rogers (center) and
John Keenan (left).

Mel Glass (right) enjoys a soda with
John Keenan in the backyard of
Glass's home in Queens.

A celebration of Mel Glass's tenure in the
DA's office and his appointment to the
bench, effective April 1973.

Richard Robles is returned to the Twenty-Third Precinct police station on East 104th Street. *(New York Daily News/Getty)*

Richard Robles, convicted murderer.
(Bettmann/Corbis /AP Images)

Mel Glass served as a criminal court judge and a justice of the New York State Supreme Court.

Mel Glass's grandchildren. Back row: Steven Zayas, Alec Glass, James Fryer, Tessa Fryer, Olivia Glass, Geoffrey Fryer. Middle row: Samantha Zayas, Patrick Glass, Peter Glass, Michael Fryer. Front: Sabrina Zayas. *(Photo by Paul Glass)*

innocent man; he didn't want to make that mistake again now. But he had no doubt that what he'd just heard was closer to the truth than anything Whitmore had confessed to doing.

"I think we've narrowed the killer down to three people," he replied. "It's either Jimmy, Margie or this guy Robles."

"What makes you say that?" Lappin asked.

"A few reasons, but the main one is that her story matches the evidence," Mel replied as he began to pace. "She corroborated her husband's account, as well as known details from the crime scene. But they both had other details that were not in any police reports, including the DD5s."

"So what's your next step?" Cavanaugh asked.

Mel thought about it for a moment. "I think I better call Herman," he said, and walked into a third office, where he dialed the home number of Homicide Bureau chief Al Herman.

When Herman came to the telephone, Glass quickly explained the situation with Delaney. "If this looks like the real deal, can I offer him immunity for his current case?"

There was a pause on the other end of the line, and then Herman said, "Sure. If it was self-defense, then we're really not giving him anything."

A few minutes later, Mel Glass was seated back at his desk, while the Delaneys and the police officers took seats at the table. He looked at Jimmy and then Margie, judging their moods. "I want to bring Robles into the office now and tell him that you just told me he's the killer."

Margie looked alarmed, but Jimmy just calmly asked, "Why?"

"Well, there are a number of reasons I'd like to have this confrontation," Mel said. "One thing is that you're going to have to testify in this case and identify him in court. I'd like to see now how he reacts to what you have to say. Plus, you're going to have to face him in that courtroom, and this will be a good first test. Are you with me?"

Jimmy and Margie Delaney looked at each other and then nodded. "Yeah, we're in," Jimmy said.

"Good," Mel replied. "But you have to promise me that whatever he says, you won't react. He will likely do one of two things. He'll probably say you're full of shit and create a drama . . . or he might confess and say you're right. I think that's unlikely but it's worth a shot. Either way, it's to our advantage."

As Glass continued talking to the Delaneys—ordering in some sandwiches and drinks as they waited—Lappin called detectives at the Twenty-third Precinct and asked them to pick up Robles at Dolly Ruiz's apartment and bring him to the DAO. The irony was not lost on Mel that for all the massive, citywide search for the killer, this suspect lived only five blocks from where Janice Wylie and Emily Hoffert were murdered—though in a dramatically less affluent neighborhood.

It was the late evening of October 19, 1964, when Richard Robles was brought to the Criminal Courts Building. Lappin met the other detectives and the suspect downstairs and then escorted them to Glass's office.

Upon seeing the Delaneys, Robles stopped abruptly. His jaw dropped and his face drained of color as he stared at the couple without speaking.

Glass used the pause to look over the young man. He didn't seem to fit the image of a killer: the twenty-year-old was clean-cut, with dark, wavy hair, dark eyes and a handsome face.

Looks can certainly be deceiving, Glass thought before matter-of-factly telling Robles that the Delaneys had just named him as the killer in the Wylie-Hoffert case.

Robles's eyes suddenly burned with rage as he looked at his accusers. "You two pieces of shit!" he yelled. "You low-life, lying motherfuckers. Jimmy, word has it that you got yourself in a crack and now you want to jack me up to get your pathetic ass out of the sling. Well, fuck you both!"

Robles suddenly turned as if to leave the office. Mel Glass jumped up from his chair and snarled, "Mr. Robles, stop right there!"

The suspect paused and then turned back to face Glass, who said, "You say the Delaneys are lying. Well, fair enough. I guess you wouldn't mind taking a lie detector test to prove it?"

Robles's jaw clenched. "I'll take your test anytime, anywhere!"

"Good," Glass said with a smile. "I'll arrange it for some time in the next week or so."

Robles glared one last time at the Delaneys; then he turned and left the room, followed by the detectives who brought him.

Mel looked at the couple. "You guys still in?"

"Yeah," Jimmy Delaney said as Margie nodded. "He's lying, Mr. Glass. He's a fuckin' liar."

"Well, it helped," Mel replied. He looked at the man sitting at the table and a thought struck his mind. "By the way, Jimmy, you know that Delaney is an old Irish family name, which may not have any relevance directly to you. But my wife, Betty, she's a nurse. She's from Ireland. So I know a little about the Emerald Isle. You know the story of St. Patrick?"

"Yeah, sure, doesn't everybody?" Delaney said with a grin. "He brought Christianity."

"That's right, and he did it without violence," Mel agreed. "He adapted by taking some of the old Celtic customs and blending them in with the practices of the Catholic Church. That's what we're going to do now, *adapt*."

"How do you mean?" Delaney asked.

"Well, I believe that Robles is going to call you as soon as you get home," Mel said.

"Why?" Delaney asked.

"Because he's going to want to know exactly what you told us," Glass replied. "You tell him you want him to come to your apartment if he wants to talk—that you don't want to talk over the phone. When he gets there, just tell him matter-of-factly that you had to name him because of your case with Cruz . . . that you had to come up with something dramatic, but that you didn't tell us much. Then say that you need to know exactly what happened at the girls' apartment—so that if we question you again, you won't accidentally give us the right details."

Delaney nodded and patted his wife on her knee. "We can do that."

As the couple got up to leave, Mel asked another question. "Jimmy, do you believe in redemption? You know, in taking advantage of a chance to make things right?"

Delaney furrowed his brow. "Yeah, I guess."

"That's good, because I believe in second chances, and I think that's what you've got here."

Nodding, Delaney said, "Yeah, I guess it is."

When the Delaneys were gone, Lappin turned to Glass, who was standing next to him, and asked, "So where do we go from here, Mel?"

Mel grinned and patted him on the shoulder. "Not to worry, I have a plan."

CHAPTER 13

A little more than a week after the confrontation with Richard Robles, Mel Glass waited for the suspect in the office of Detective Nat Laurendi, a polygraph expert for the NYPD assigned to the DAO. It was midmorning, and it didn't surprise him that Robles was late for his appointment with the lie detector. Glass thought it was just as likely that the young man wouldn't show at all.

Glass got his answer when Detective Paddy Lappin's large body hurtled into the room. The big man's face was red from exertion and his light blue eyes were bright with anger.

"Robles's dad just called me. Our guy OD'd last night," Lappin snarled. "Some of his junkie friends found him unconscious. He's in a coma at Metropolitan Hospital and might not make it!"

Glass blinked once and stood up. "Let's go," he said, and headed out the door. "If we're lucky, maybe we get a deathbed confession."

"We'll take my car," Lappin said as they got on the elevator.

If Robles died now, they'd never learn the truth, nor have the satisfaction of bringing him to justice for the murders of Janice

125

Wylie and Emily Hoffert. And George Whitmore would still be on the hook for crimes he didn't commit. The Delaneys' stories corroborated each other's, but they were junkies with criminal records—facts a defense attorney was sure to exploit. He needed Richard Robles to corroborate them and implicate himself.

As the elevator reached the ground floor, they walked quickly down Baxter Street, where Lappin had parked his unmarked squad car. Climbing in, Glass prayed, *Please let him be alive when we get there. . . .*

Lappin glanced over at Glass and knew what was going through the ADA's mind. "Don't worry," he tried to assure his friend, "junkies don't die at Metropolitan."

"I hope you're right, Paddy," Mel replied quietly as he turned to look out the side window.

As Paddy Lappin sped down Grand Street, heading for First Avenue, Mel Glass noted that the once-brilliant foliage of the maples, oaks and elms in Sara D. Roosevelt Park appeared to be on its last legs. The month of October was drawing to an end, and the pedestrians, hurrying through the chill morning, pulled their coats around them and clutched hats to their heads.

On a national level, it was a month that would be a snapshot of a rapidly changing America. During a trip to assess an escalating military "situation" in Vietnam, Secretary of Defense Robert McNamara declared that the United States would "stay as long as it takes" to defeat the Communists in the North. In Stockholm, Martin Luther King Jr. was awarded the Nobel Peace Prize. In Philadelphia, Mississippi, the FBI located the bodies of three missing civil rights workers, who had been on a mission to register disenfranchised blacks to vote, but were murdered, instead, by local law enforcement and members of the KKK.

At Madison Square Garden, President Lyndon B. Johnson announced a set of domestic social programs he called "the Great

Society" whose purpose was to "eliminate poverty and racial injustice." However, the big news in the five boroughs was that the Yankees had lost in the seventh game of the World Series to St. Louis, throwing the team's legions of fans into a pin-striped funk. Mel Glass, an inveterate Phillies fan, was not among the mourners.

Media interest in the "Career Girls Murders" had waned, despite the fact that Whitmore was slated for a November trial in Brooklyn for the Estrada attempted rape/assault. It seemed that with George's arrest and indictment for the Wylie-Hoffert murders, the public and press were satisfied that the case was solved and life could go on, now that George "Brooklyn Psycho" Whitmore was safely off the streets.

Only a very few people knew that was not true—that the killer was still out there among them.

As Lappin turned left and sped north on First Avenue, heading for Metro Hospital on Ninety-seventh Street, Mel thought about what he'd learned since first meeting Richard Robles. After the confrontation between Robles and the Delaneys, Mel had tried to get a couple of hours' sleep on one of the office couches. When others started arriving in the office for the day, he got up and talked to Homicide Bureau chief Al Herman again, asking to have the charges against Jimmy Delaney dropped. He then called and eventually got in touch with Detective David Downes.

At the time of the murders in August 1963, Downes was assigned to the 107th Precinct in Queens. But as he recalled for Glass, in 1960 he'd been working out of the Two-Three for twelve years when he apprehended the then-sixteen-year-old Richard "Ricky" Robles, who was wanted for burglary and sexual assault.

The kid was already a career criminal. "We figured he was good for maybe a hundred break-ins," Downes told Glass.

Robles had "the face of a choirboy," but a violent temper. "We could never pin it on him, but we know he shot a pawnshop owner for trying to lowball him on a piece of expensive jewelry he was trying to hawk," Downes shared with Glass.

Nor was Robles the sort of burglar who liked to slip in and out of his victims' homes or offices without leaving a trace, or even unnoticed. He seemed to enjoy ransacking apartments and destroying property he wasn't taking with him, like the time he broke into a lawyer's home and slashed the clothing he found in the man's closet.

Most of all, or so he'd told some of his criminal associates, he got a "kick" out of terrorizing the women he sometimes encountered—tying them up and threatening them with knives.

"He's said he enjoys watching their eyes as he terrorizes them," Downes recalled.

However, Robles wasn't all just threats. When a woman he'd once surprised in her apartment was too slow removing a ring he demanded, he'd seized her hand and ripped it off her finger. He'd also sexually assaulted the woman—though he'd stopped short of raping her.

There was another facet about the 1960 sexual assault/burglary case that alerted Downes when he heard some of the details about the Wylie-Hoffert murders in the first week of September 1963.

"In the 1960 case, Robles climbed in through a window at about eleven in the morning," he recalled for Glass.

Following his arrest by Downes, Robles had been convicted and sentenced to five years in the Elmira Reformatory. However, when the Wylie-Hoffert case went down three years later, the detective had no idea where the violent young burglar was—in or out of Elmira. When Downes talked to his commander, Lieutenant Ray Jones, about his suspicions, Jones suggested that he check to see if Robles was on the streets. If Robles was,

Downes should call the detective squad at the Two-Three with his tip.

Sure enough, Downes learned that Robles had been released from Elmira in June 1963, having been let go early "for good behavior." The detective immediately notified the Two-Three detectives who were working Wylie-Hoffert. He told them he thought they ought to look at Robles for several reasons: Robles was known for working that area of the Upper East Side; he entered apartments during the day by climbing into open windows; he had a penchant for violence and sexual assault, in addition to burglary. In response to Downes's tip, two parole officers were sent out to find Robles and bring him into the Twenty-third Precinct.

As it turned out, the detectives who questioned Robles were John Lynch and Marty Zinkand. When they asked Robles where he'd been on the morning of August 28, the teen at first said he couldn't remember. But under continued questioning, he suddenly recalled that he'd been mopping and sweeping the apartment building where his mother was the manager. The detectives immediately tried to contact Robles's mother, but she wasn't in. Several days later, when they did reach her—and after the suspect had time to talk to her—she backed up her son's story.

In hindsight Ricky Robles stood out as a prime suspect. But at the time, he'd been just one of hundreds of potential suspects—burglars, rapists, murderers—pulled in by the police for questioning, many of them with no better alibis than the teenager. As such, the DD5 report from Lynch and Zinkand had gone into the task force files like all the others.

After talking to Detective Downes, Glass had tried to find out as much as he could about Robles. He'd talked to the parole office and counselors at Elmira, and the detectives had hit the streets, interviewing Robles's friends and colleagues in crime. The picture that emerged was much more in line with the profile Glass's psychologist sister, Blanche, had painted of the killer.

The seeds for Richard Robles's anger and his drug addiction had been planted in childhood and nurtured through his early teens. He'd grown up in the Yorkville area of Manhattan, which was poor, crime-ridden and violent. Although still technically the Upper East Side, Yorkville was a much different and much harsher environment than the more affluent areas he would later victimize. His father had been a heavy drinker and abusive, while his mother openly carried on an affair with the husband of a woman named Dolly Ruiz, the aunt of one Margie Delaney. Perhaps out of revenge, Dolly began having sex with Ricky, who was only fifteen at the time, already a heroin addict and fifteen years her junior. Almost two years later, they had a daughter together; but before the child's first birthday, Robles had been sent off to Elmira.

Of the street people the detectives talked to, one in particular interested Mel Glass. He was an old small-time crook named Leo Wallace, who like Fagin in *Oliver Twist* claimed to have taught Robles the art of being a cat burglar. His specialty had been the "daytime stepover"—using a ledge or windowsill to reach over to climb in through open windows at times when the apartment dwellers were likely to be at work.

However, Robles apparently wasn't too worried about the residents, particularly if they were young females.

"Wallace once saw him on East Seventy-seventh and Park Avenue waiting to hit an apartment," Lynch reported to Glass. "Wallace asked him why he wasn't going in, and Robles said he was—and I quote—'waiting for the chick to come back to the apartment' first."

Hearing about Wallace's comments, Glass thought about what Downes had said regarding Robles's entering apartments through windows during daylight hours, and Lynch's report from the crime scene of seeing the kitchen window open. One of the big questions regarding Whitmore's confession was that he said— with Detective Bulger's prompting—that he entered the service stairwell leading to the apartment through the door in the lobby. But Glass had gone over to the building himself and established that the door in the lobby leading to the service stairwell always clicked and locked shut, and could only be opened from the stairwell side. Yet, according to Bulger, Whitmore had somehow managed to open a locked door, bearing no sign, and leading to God knows where, all the while slipping past the doorman. It seemed questionable.

Occam's razor again, Glass thought, *the simplest explanation is usually the right one.*

As the Whitmore case unraveled, Mel Glass tried to warn the Brooklyn DA and Brooklyn cops about the real possibility that the Whitmore confessions in the Estrada and Edmonds cases were likely suspect. Since the confession in Wylie-Hoffert was worthless, Glass advised that Brooklyn better be able to corroborate with independent evidence everything that George Whitmore Jr. had to say.

The Brooklyn response had been that if the New York DAO wanted to "chase rainbows," that was Hogan's business. They had an airtight case that included a positive identification of Whitmore by Estrada, and a solid confession that would hold up in court. The prosecution of George Whitmore Jr. was going forward, beginning with the Estrada case in the first week of November '64 to be followed by the Edmonds murder case in the spring of '65.

In New York County, Hogan wasn't ready to drop the charges against George Whitmore Jr. and indict Richard Robles. There were several issues that needed to be resolved first. It wasn't enough that the New York DAO was convinced that Whitmore was innocent of the Wylie-Hoffert murders, they were going to have to do everything in their power to prove it. After all, a Manhattan grand jury, based on the evidence presented to it, handed down an indictment. Certainly, that fact was bound to be used against them by Robles's defense attorney, who'd label the People's case "a fishing expedition" and argue that when the DAO came to the conclusion that it could not convict Whitmore, it had to find another patsy and did so in the poor, young Richard Robles.

So part of Glass's challenge was to be able to thwart that attack by essentially destroying the DAO's own initial case against George Whitmore Jr. Exposing the photograph as a fraud was dynamite, but Glass and his detectives had not stopped there.

Ever since their first meeting, Glass had stayed in contact with Whitmore's mom, Bernadine. Through her, the detectives had found Ludie Montgomery, who fondly recalled her friendship with George. She said that during August '63, they'd met in Wildwood in the Ivy Hotel lobby, where he used to hang out to watch the famous musicians who stayed and performed there. It wasn't much of a romance; after all, she was only fifteen. Their dates mostly consisted of innocently sipping sodas together in the lobby, people-watching and staring at a small black-and-white television in the corner.

Then Ludie dropped her bombshell. She didn't think George could have committed the murders, because she'd met him in the lobby at seven-thirty in the evening of August 28. She was positive of the time and date because they'd watched a television newscast of Martin Luther King Jr. delivering his "I Have a Dream" speech.

Ludie recalled that her friend was excited by what he'd heard in King's speech, though he'd admitted that he didn't understand all of what the civil rights leader was talking about. But, otherwise, he didn't seem agitated or frightened, as one might expect of a double murderer, nor did he mention going to New York City that day.

The young woman's story was confirmed by her mother, Jenny Montgomery, who in a separate interview said she'd also seen Whitmore sitting with her daughter in the lobby the night of King's speech. Further investigation turned up Larry Wilson, a seventeen-year-old student at Wildwood High and a dishwasher at the Ivy, who'd drifted out to the lobby to listen to King and saw Whitmore.

It wasn't an airtight alibi. George Whitmore could have been in New York on the morning of August 28, murdered two women, made his way back to Wildwood, traveling over 130 miles in several hours, arriving that evening in time for the news. But it was not the simplest or the correct explanation, Glass knew.

By mid-October, Mel Glass had essentially everything the prosecution would need to demonstrate to a jury why the DAO had decided upon further investigation that George Whitmore Jr. was not the killer. Still, given the unique circumstances of the case, he didn't want to tip his hand by dismissing the indictment against Whitmore.

While committed to the ideal that the unjustly accused must be exonerated, Glass knew that an immediate dismissal of the indictment would not free Whitmore. The Kings County, Brooklyn, DAO had Whitmore remanded—no bail—on the Edmonds murder and Estrada attempted rape/assault cases.

More important, Glass wanted to build the case against the killer. He believed that as long as Whitmore was still the indicted defendant, Richard Robles might slip up. And they needed him to slip up; right now it was Robles's word against the Delaneys'.

That was the inducing cause for Glass to put his plan into action after he interviewed the Delaneys. He'd asked Jimmy and

Margie to continue trying to get Robles to talk about the murder. Hopefully, Robles would drop some more evidentiary nuggets that would further implicate him.

What he didn't tell the Delaneys was that he'd persuaded Hogan to sign off on court-ordered "bugging" of their apartment, without their knowledge. With the cooperation of the New York Fire Department (FDNY), the Delaney apartment building was evacuated under the ruse that a fire had been reported. As tenants of the dingy brick five-story walk-up filed out onto the street, a contingent of firefighters and DAO wiremen rushed in. As the firefighters made a show of looking for a fire, which didn't exist, the DAO technicians planted a microphone on a top shelf of the living-room closet. Meanwhile, a listening post was set up in an apartment a block away.

In the few weeks that followed, the Delaneys had tried several times to get Robles to incriminate himself by talking about the Wylie-Hoffert case. Most of the time, Robles danced around their questions or made innocuous statements, which did little to build the case against him. Occasionally he said things that could be interpreted as incriminating, but even then the recordings were of such poor quality that they would be of questionable value in a courtroom.

Paddy Lappin finally pulled the sedan up to the curb in front of Metropolitan Hospital. Both men entered and made their way to Ward 7A. There they were informed by the attending physician that Richard Robles was admitted at nine-thirty in the evening, the night before. He was brought in by ambulance, unconscious and in a coma from an overdose of drugs.

"He's in and out of it," the doctor said. "But even when he's awake, he's not very lucid, so I don't know what you're going to get out of him."

As the doctor walked away, Lappin nudged Glass. "Maybe I should dress up like the Devil and go to his room," he said with a grin. "Then when he wakes up, tell him he's going to hell unless he confesses."

Mel laughed. "It might work," he replied. "But I think he's going to hell, no matter what he says."

CHAPTER 14

Paddy Lappin was right about junkies not dying at Metropolitan Hospital, at least not in this case. In fact, just a few days later, Richard Robles was sitting up in bed and alert when Detective David Downes dropped by his hospital room.

The handsome young junkie looked up in surprise. "Hey, Downsey, you son of a bitch, how are you?"

"I'm good, Ricky. How ya doin'?"

"Well, I'm gettin' out tomorrow," Robles replied; then he looked suspiciously at the detective. "What are you doin' here?"

Downes shrugged. "I've been assigned to Manhattan on an investigation," he replied. He didn't elaborate; but because of Downes's personal knowledge of Richard Robles, Mel Glass had asked that he be assigned to the DAO to work on the Wylie-Hoffert case.

"I thought you were in Queens."

Nonplussed, the detective replied, "How'd you know?"

"I read about the big case where you went over to Paris and came back with the doctor," Robles said with a smile.

Downes nodded. An uncomfortable silence followed, until

Robles cleared his throat and said, "You know, they're trying to frame me over here." His eyes were pleading to be believed.

When Downes looked at him, however, the detective saw past the boyish good looks. He knew there was something dark beneath the self-righteous veneer—a demon. "They're looking for the truth, Ricky," he replied, and left the room.

On the same day, George Whitmore Jr. went on trial in Brooklyn Criminal Court, charged with trying to rape and assault Alma Estrada. He and his defense team—experienced attorneys who'd volunteered to take up his cause—were up against a stacked deck from the beginning. Few people in Brooklyn didn't know that Whitmore was the media-dubbed "Brooklyn Psycho," who'd been charged with the most infamous murders in anyone's memory. A fair trial with an unbiased jury was highly unlikely.

During the prosecution case, Estrada took the stand and talked about the night in April that a man had come up from behind and grabbed her as she was walking home in the dark. She recounted the struggle, including how she'd pulled a button from her assailant's coat. And as she fought him off in the alley, she'd turned and got a good look at him. "I saw his complete face," she told the jury.

Asked if that man was in the courtroom—and if so, could she identify him—Estrada turned and pointed at George Whitmore. "That's him," she testified. "I'm sure of it."

The prosecution had also called Officer Tommy Micelli, Detective Louie Ayala and Detective Joseph DiPrima to the stand. The officer and the detectives described what led to Whitmore's apprehension and his confession, as well as identifying a raincoat, which he'd been wearing when brought in for questioning, that was missing a button.

Although unusual and risky as it left their client open to cross-examination, the defense attorneys knew that the only way to combat the impact of the confession was to put George Whitmore Jr. on the stand. The shy, inarticulate teenager, with the acne-covered face and weak eyes, made a poor witness. He mumbled his answers and had difficulty looking the jurors in their eyes, or even his own attorney's eyes, as he was questioned. That made him seem evasive.

Whitmore haltingly denied attacking Estrada and said he'd merely seen a man running, with a police officer chasing him and shooting his gun. "I was trying to help," he said of his conversation with Patrolman Micelli in the Laundromat.

The things he admitted to in his confession weren't true, he said, but he'd been afraid of the detectives. Every time he'd denied one of their accusations, he'd been shoved or hit, and then called a liar. "I continuously got beat until I couldn't take it no more," he complained, "so I just broke down and shook my head."

However, the jurors weren't going to take his word over that of NYPD's finest. It took them nine hours of deliberation, but they found him guilty of attempted rape and assault. The jubilant Brooklyn DAO viewed it as a trial run; next up was Whitmore's trial for the murder of Minnie Edmonds, for which he might face the death penalty.

When Mel Glass heard about the verdict, he shook his head. It had not mattered to the Brooklyn DAO that Whitmore's confession in Wylie-Hoffert was demonstrably false. All the prosecution had cared about was a conviction. He thought about his conversation with Dr. Morris at Bellevue back in July and how Whitmore reacted when confronted by angry authority figures: *"By saying whatever it takes to remove the cause of the stress."*

Glass didn't believe that George Whitmore Jr. was any guiltier of the Estrada and Edmonds crimes than he was culpable for the Wylie-Hoffert murders. But there was nothing Glass could do for him now—except help gather the incriminating evidence that would lead inexorably to convict the individual who had slaughtered Janice Wylie and Emily Hoffert: Richard Robles.

Efforts to tape the Delaneys' discussion of the murders with suspect Ricky Robles had met with limited success throughout November and December. Not only had Robles been cagey, but the recordings themselves were barely audible.

There had been one moment that was both amusing and alarming. Shortly before Christmas, Margie Delaney had discovered the bug in her closet while hunting for holiday decorations to put up. The Delaneys had demanded to know why they'd been bugged.

Mel Glass assured them it was for their protection—in case Robles decided he didn't like their line of questioning and got violent. The couple had looked at each other, shrugged and decided it might be a good idea.

Now with their consent, the recording strategy continued into early January '65. One day DAO investigator Phil Robinson happened to be passing Glass's office as the latter was trying to decipher a nearly unintelligible conversation among Jimmy and Margie Delaney and Ricky Robles. Robinson suggested that Glass let him install a new, technologically advanced microphone, which had much better capabilities. The new listening device was soon installed, and the apartment next door to the Delaneys' abode—occupied at the time by a police officer's mother, who was moved to a new location—became the new listening center.

The new system resulted in better-quality recordings. However, for the most part, Robles remained elusive when answering questions about the murders. Yet, here and there, he let some things slip that corroborated the Delaneys' account and locked Robles into the murders.

Piece by piece, the case against Robles was building. Still, two events at the end of January 1965 forced the New York DAO to move. The first was a story that appeared on Sunday, January 24, in the *Daily News*. The paper reported that the DAO and NYPD were looking at a "strong new suspect" in the Wylie-Hoffert murders. The story claimed that the suspect was a "22-year-old junkie ex-convict" named "Ricky." And if that wasn't enough to alarm the public, the story claimed that the alleged killer was now armed with a gun.

The reporter didn't name his main source for the story, but it was clear that whoever gave him the details was a ranking police officer with intimate knowledge of the case. Manhattan NYPD brass was getting impatient and had been pressing for the arrest of Richard Robles. Officially, the only response to the story from the DAO and NYPD was that the murder investigation was continuing, but that George Whitmore Jr. was still under indictment.

The second event took place on the morning of January 26. Mel Glass was in his office when the telephone rang. It was Jimmy Delaney, who said that Robles was planning to commit an armed robbery that night. The young killer had wanted Delaney to participate, but he'd made an excuse and then called Glass.

Telling Delaney to hang tight at his apartment, Glass then called Frank Hogan. If someone got hurt during the robbery—and the DAO had known it was going to happen and had done nothing to prevent it—there'd be hell to pay.

Reaching his boss, Mel quickly explained what was going on and was told to come to the DA's office. He arrived in the reception room about noon. Ida Delaney, Hogan's secretary, was already standing at the door of Hogan's inner office. "They're expecting you," she said, and opened the door.

Wondering who "they" were, Mel walked in. Along with Frank Hogan, Homicide Bureau chief Al Herman and Hogan's executive assistant, ADA Dave Worgan, were seated in the room. Pointing to the chair directly in front of his desk, Hogan said, "Have a seat, Mel, and tell us what you've learned."

Glass got right to the point. He went over Delaney's telephone call and voiced his concern that the newspaper story might have made Richard Robles more desperate. "He's under a lot of stress, and he could go off on somebody tonight," he said.

As the young ADA spoke, Hogan had filled his pipe and now lit it before speaking. "I agree," he said at last. "The question is, what, then?"

Glass started to speak, but then he hesitated. What he was going to suggest next was a big step—the culmination of everything he'd worked for since reading the entire case file back in late June '64. But it also had far-reaching implications.

"I think it's time to indict him for the murders of Janice Wylie and Emily Hoffert," Glass proposed.

Silence enveloped the room. Every man there knew that indicting Robles for the same crimes they'd indicted Whitmore—but not as a co-conspirator or accomplice—was going to invite a firestorm of criticism for the DAO and the NYPD. However, the ramifications went beyond that.

In January 1965, while authorities including the police were being challenged and accused of corruption and malfeasance in other American cities, the honest law-abiding citizens of the five boroughs still admired and respected the New York Police Department. As Whitmore's trial in Brooklyn had recently proved, if the guilt or innocence of a defendant was a contest between the testimony of the police and that of the accused, jurors almost always gave the NYPD the benefit of the doubt.

Now, if it was shown that police detectives were less than truthful and coerced false confessions, it meant the entire justice system would be seriously eroded. And that meant that the New York DAO would also suffer an enormous blow to its hard-earned reputation and the public trust.

Dave Worgan and Al Herman both suggested that it might not be wise to dismiss the indictment against Whitmore. "It could adversely affect the Brooklyn cases," Worgan said. "It shows that we don't believe the Whitmore confession, which could taint the Brooklyn confessions as well."

Resting his elbows on his armchair, Hogan leaned forward. "So we keep an indictment pending against Whitmore, whom we believe to be an innocent man, to help law enforcement in Brooklyn?" He bowed his head and shook it. Then he stood and walked around his desk, which he leaned against, facing his two senior advisers. "I'm having a lot of trouble understanding your point of view. It was one thing strategically not to dismiss against Whitmore, while trying to corroborate the Delaneys and, hopefully, do it with admissions from Robles. Fortunately, now we have some corroboration from those conversations. But we didn't dismiss initially against Whitmore as he was being held without bail on the Brooklyn cases. Also a dismissal may have alarmed Robles and he might have fled. Now we're going to lock Robles up, and I can't imagine not exonerating Whitmore at the same time. Not to do so would compromise who we are and what we do."

Hogan paused; then he resumed his seat. "As chief law enforcement officer, I believe there is a major moral dimension to our job." Suddenly he pounded his fist on the desk. "Let's face it. We blundered by indicting Whitmore. We're not going to compound the initial mistake by playing questionable games with the system to help convict someone in Brooklyn who may very well be innocent. In court we rightfully have the burden of proof—that's as it should be. The system is tilted in favor of the prosecution. We *should* win our cases after trial. Why not? We're like the '27 Yankees, so we don't gloat in victory. Remember, we sum up last. We can explain to the court and jury why our case is honest and rebut with the facts and evidence the insincere defense. Well, here again, we are the last voice. As long as I sit here as DA, we'll do justice, even if we have to admit we were wrong at the outset. . . . Mel, what do you think?" The D.A. turned to his young protégé, placing his pipe in his mouth as he settled back in his chair.

Mel hesitated. Collectively, the men sitting with him had one hundred years' more experience than he did. But he was no shrinking violet when he felt he was right. "There's not much I can add to what you just said," he began, addressing Hogan. "You, with the senior members of this office, have worked extremely hard to establish your reputation. If we don't dismiss Whitmore now, I think your credibility will be severely damaged."

Hogan smiled as he removed the pipe from his mouth and pointed the stem at Glass. "That's what I thought you'd say. So go forth and do justice, Mel. Do justice."

CHAPTER 15

When Mel Glass announced that it was time to move on Robles, the team of detectives sprang into action. They'd kept the suspect under surveillance, including using a fake yellow taxicab from which to follow his movements on the streets. Therefore, Detective Marty Zinkand knew where to find Robles as he stood on the corner of East Eighty-ninth Street and Third Avenue. The big detective pounced on Robles before the suspect realized he was a cop.

"What's this about?" Robles demanded as the detective placed the handcuffs over his thin wrists.

"You're under arrest," Zinkand snarled, "for the murders of Janice Wylie and Emily Hoffert."

As Robles pleaded his innocence, the fake cab drove up. Zinkand hauled his "collar" over to the curb and pushed him down into the backseat. Like a regular cop car, the taxi had no handles allowing escape. The car proceeded to the northeast corner of Ninety-third Street and Third Avenue, where Lieutenant Cavanaugh and Sergeant William Brent entered the vehicle.

Instead of taking Robles straight to the Twenty-third

Precinct, they removed the handcuffs and drove around for about an hour questioning the suspect, who denied being involved in the Wylie-Hoffert murders. At one point Cavanaugh told Robles, "This is D-day."

Robles then reached into his pocket and pulled out a business card for attorney Mack Dollinger. "I want to speak to my lawyer," he said.

The investigators ignored his request and instead drove him over to the Delaneys' second-floor apartment on 330 East Eighty-fourth Street. The couple was home and met the detectives and Robles at the door. Suddenly realizing why he'd been brought to the apartment, Robles again demanded to see a lawyer.

Jimmy Delaney rushed up to Robles. Before the police could move, Delaney jabbed his index finger into the suspect's chest. "Fuck a lawyer, Ricky! Everything you've said here has been recorded! We've been working with the DA's office and the cops. They know everything! They've heard your voice! Your only chance not to fry in Sing Sing is to tell the truth and cooperate."

Blinking in shock, Robles stared at Jimmy Delaney—his supplier, fellow addict and friend. But there was no pity there.

"He's right, girl killer," Margie sneered. "We've been cooperating. The apartment is bugged and taped. So much for us being the liars."

If Robles needed any more convincing, Cavanaugh led him over to the closet and showed him the microphone. "We've recorded everything you've said in here for the past three months," the lieutenant informed him. "Now, why don't you make this easier on yourself and talk to us about killing those girls."

Robles's face turned white and he burst into tears. "I'm sorry I'm not dead," he cried. "I tried to kill myself. Jail is a horrible place, where you just rot. I need a shot, Jimmy, and then I'll talk. . . ." But then his voice trailed off, and he refused to say anything more without his lawyer.

* * *

For three hours the detectives questioned Robles at the Delaney apartment. But although he would bend—while alternating between asking to see a lawyer and pleading for a shot of heroin—he wouldn't break and confess outright. Finally Lieutenant Cavanaugh decided it was time to take him to the Twenty-third Precinct headquarters to be booked.

About the same time as the suspect and his captors left the Delaney apartment, Glass drove away from the Criminal Courts Building and headed uptown to the Twenty-third Precinct, too. When he arrived, he moved past the press, who'd heard rumors of an arrest in Wylie-Hoffert. He made his way to the detective squad room on the second floor, where Robles was being held in a detention cage.

Detective Zinkand walked over to brief him on what had happened at the Delaney apartment. The detective had just finished, when another officer approached. Looking at Glass, he hooked a thumb behind his back at Robles. "He wants to see you alone."

Glass excused himself from Zinkand and walked over to the detention cage. "I understand you asked to talk to me?"

"Yeah," Robles replied. He hesitated a moment, licking his thin blue lips, and scratching incessantly at his arms. When he looked up at Glass, the suspect's eyes were frightened, pleading. "What can you do for me?" he asked.

Glass didn't answer right away. He stood for a moment reminding himself that this scared, drug-addicted young man was also a vicious murderer. Then Glass spoke: "It's not what I can do for you, Ricky. It's what you can do for yourself. You have obviously been living with this for a long time, so you might as well get it off your chest. Make a clean breast of things."

"What about psychiatric help?"

Glass shrugged. "Right now, it is a black-and-white situation. The cops say you did it, and you say you didn't do it. We have nothing to base psychiatric help on. Maybe if you give a full statement for the court, it can be presented to a judge and a psychiatrist to analyze and determine if you need psychiatric help."

Robles sat still, except for his rapidly blinking eyes. So Glass pushed a little harder. "It appears you panicked in the apartment."

"It wasn't panic. Something went wrong."

"Do you want to tell me about it?" asked Glass, much more nonchalantly than he felt.

Robles started to say something, but then he closed his mouth. Suddenly Mack Dollinger hurried into the squad room. The suspect nodded toward him. "I want to speak to my lawyer first."

Glass glanced over his shoulder at the defense attorney. "I'll go get him," he said.

Detective David Downes arrived at the Twenty-third Precinct about the same time after receiving a call from Mel Glass, who'd let him know about the arrest. He'd hurried out of his house in Yonkers and drove into Manhattan. Reaching the Two-Three—which was abuzz with news about the Robles bust, with brass hurrying every which way—he quietly made his way to the detective squad room on the second floor. He spotted Glass standing with Dollinger, a tall, handsome Clark Kent type. Downes walked over.

Glass looked at him and asked him to take Robles over to the clerical office so that the defendant could speak to his lawyer, Dollinger. The defense attorney remained in the office with Robles for about a half hour and then emerged. "Detective, would you mind staying with him while I go talk to Mel?"

Downes watched as Dollinger and Glass engaged in an animated conversation, and then Downes walked into the office where Robles sat. The suspect looked terrible. His eyes were feverish and haunted; his face and trembling hands were a sickly pallor. He scratched at his arms as though every inch itched. The detective thought about the first time he'd seen him in 1960—a nice-looking sixteen-year-old, but already a drug addict and career criminal.

"How ya doin', Ricky?" Downes asked.

Robles grimaced. "I need a fix," he said. "The last time I shot up was two in the morning. I'm jonesing for a hit, man."

Ignoring the comment, Downes shook his head. "Boy, Ricky, did you ever think it would end up like this? You're twenty-one years old and you've made a real mess of your life. What really happened?"

Robles dropped his head and then began to nod. He looked up with tears welling in his eyes. "I don't know, Downes. I went to pull a lousy burglary and I wound up killing two girls."

CHAPTER 16

October 18, 1965

"All rise! Put down your papers in the back."

At the command of the portly, bespectacled court clerk, a wide array of attorneys, the defendant, clerks, cops, reporters, media sketch artists, photographers, court buffs and gawkers jumped up from their seats as a burly, round-faced, black-robed judge swept into the courtroom. They remained at near attention as he climbed the dais and took his seat. His stern gaze swept over the assembly.

"Oyez, oyez, oyez!" the clerk continued a bit pompously, as fitting the occasion of this particular trial. "All those who having business before Part thirty-nine of the Supreme Court, State of New York, New York County, draw near and ye shall be heard. The Honorable Supreme Court justice Irwin D. Davidson presiding. The case on trial, *the People of the State of New York* versus *the Defendant, Richard Robles,* ready to proceed."

The clerk paused for a moment and scanned from one side of the courtroom to the other to make sure everyone was paying attention. Satisfied, he continued, "Representing the People, the Honorable Assistant District Attorney John Keenan and Assistant District Attorney Melvin Glass. Representing the defendant,

Mr. Mack Dollinger and Mr. Frank Backer. Your Honor, all counsel, the jury and the defendant are present."

Having delivered his traditional introductions with the finesse of a Shakespearean actor on Broadway, the clerk turned to the judge and nodded once. Judge Davidson, a seasoned jurist who had presided over some of the most horrendous cases in the city, smiled briefly at his longtime clerk's added flair before his face grew grave again.

"Be seated," the judge instructed.

As the jurors somberly filed into the jury box, Mel Glass looked around the courtroom, a large, bleak chamber devoid of any adornments other than the flags of the United States and New York State in one corner. The well of the courtroom was covered with a worn red carpet upon which sat the judge's dais at the far end in the middle, with the witness stand and jury box on the judge's left. Also in the "well," the prosecution table adjacent to the jury box, where Glass sat, was to the judge's left; the defense table was across the aisle on Davidson's right.

Behind the prosecution and defense tables was the bar, a wooden rail separating the well from the gallery, where everyone else sat. There was room for eighty-four spectators in Part 39, the official designation of that particular courtroom on the thirteenth floor of the Criminal Courts Building. The first row behind the attorneys on either side was reserved for family of the defendant and defense team's assistants, as well as the family of the victims and police personnel and press. The remaining seats were filled to capacity with spectators that morning.

The first day of the trial for the "Career Girls Murders" had the feel of opening night on the Great White Way. Although muted now, before the judge came in, the gallery had been buzzing as reporters joked and argued among themselves; civilians, some of whom had brought bag lunches and reading material, gossiped with their neighbors and craned their necks to get a look at the defendant and the other actors in the real-life drama.

Perched on the edge of his seat next to Glass, one of the most senior assistant district attorneys in the Homicide Bureau, John Keenan, pored one last time over the notes for his opening statement. Though not physically imposing—in fact, slight of stature with a receding hairline—Keenan was nevertheless intellectually intimidating in a courtroom, virtually magical in his ability to control the tempo and rhythm of a trial. He had a captivating presence, having a well-earned reputation as one of the best trial lawyers in the country. He would be lead counsel handling the presentation of the prosecution case, while Glass's duties as second chair were to assist primarily with trial strategy and knowing in intricate detail the entire investigative process and factual underpinnings of the case.

While Judge Davidson instructed the twelve jurors, plus four alternates, on what to expect in the trial and their responsibilities, Mel Glass reflected on the past year. As expected, the DAOs on both sides of the East River had been immediately engulfed by the maelstrom that followed the announcement of the Robles arrest, and the subsequent press barrage. The newspapers and television broadcasts reported that Robles had confessed, which suddenly put Whitmore's contentions that he'd been coerced into making a false confession—and the justice system in New York—in a whole new light. One paper kept referring to the George Whitmore Jr. "snafu"; and that was one of the kinder editorial comments.

An anonymous prosecutor was quoted in a newspaper shortly after the arrest of Richard Robles: *"I am positive that the police prepared the confession for Whitmore. They gave Whitmore all the details of the killings."*

The public was confused and angry—especially the black community, which was incensed that white police detectives might have framed an innocent young black man. The Brooklyn chapter of the National Association for the Advancement of Colored

People (NAACP) asked Governor Nelson Rockefeller to intervene in the case and "use your good offices in the interest of justice."

The Brooklyn DA dug his head in the sand and responded by saying the New York DAO was free to make its own decisions, but his office was sure of the legitimacy of its cases. The Wylie-Hoffert case was a Manhattan headache, not Brooklyn's. In the meantime, he noted, Whitmore had been found guilty of attempted rape and assault in the Alma Estrada trial by an impartial jury, which had looked at the evidence. His office would be going forward with Whitmore's trial for the slaying of Minnie Edmonds.

However, the Brooklyn DAO suffered a blow in March '65 when Whitmore's conviction for the Estrada mugging was overturned. It had come to the attention of the presiding judge that during deliberations some of the jurors had made racist remarks and, although warned not to, they had also discussed the fact that the defendant had been indicted for the Wylie-Hoffert murders. The jurors were questioned, after which the judge vacated the guilty verdict, writing, *The hearing revealed that prejudice and racial bias invaded the jury room. Bigotry in any of its sinister forms is reprehensible; it must be crushed.*

Again, the Brooklyn DA wasn't caving in. He promptly declared that his office would retry Whitmore for the Estrada assault. And, as promised, George Whitmore Jr. went on trial for the Edmonds murder in April '65, with the possibility of the death penalty hanging above his head.

At George Whitmore Jr.'s trial, both sides would discuss the Wylie-Hoffert case, which had happened in Manhattan. In a pretrial hearing, defense attorney Harry Hart attempted to keep Whitmore's confession to the Edmonds murder out of the trial. Arguing in front of the judge, he noted what had happened with the Wylie-Hoffert case across the river in Manhattan. But the prosecutors countered that even if Whitmore's confession in the Wylie-Hoffert case was false—a point they were not conceding—that didn't mean his confessions in the Estrada and Edmonds cases were as well.

The judge presiding over the Edmonds trial sided with the prosecutors. He said that the confession could be read to the jurors, and it would be up to them to decide if it was trustworthy or not. After the judge announced his ruling, Hart cried out, "Your Honor, my client is doomed by this decision!"

It was a momentous decision, however, for the Brooklyn DAO. What little the prosecutors had in physical evidence from the Edmonds murder scene couldn't be tied to Whitmore. Their entire case rested on the confession and the testimony of Officer Micelli and Detectives Ayala and DiPrima, who took the stand and recounted the arrest and confession of the suspect. And, they maintained, there was no coercion, nor did they provide Whitmore with details of the case in order to make his confession appear to be true.

On April 23, almost a year to the day since he was taken into custody, George Whitmore Jr. climbed up on the witness stand. Speaking slowly, but deliberately, he answered his attorney's questions about the circumstances of his confession and why it was false. He said that the only information he had about the killings was what the detectives had told him. Then he spent two days sticking to his story while the prosecution tried to tear him down and trip him up, without much success.

In his summation defense attorney Hart accused the police of a frame-up. "When Wylie-Hoffert blew up, it left them with a little egg on their face," he complained to the jury. "There's only one way to wipe it off, and that's to convict him for something else."

In response the prosecutor's summation argued that Whitmore confessed to the crime and there was no evidence to suggest that he'd been beaten or otherwise physically coerced into his admissions. There was also no evidence, according to the prosecutor, that the detectives fed Whitmore the details that "only the killer could have known."

The jury then deliberated for more than four days, without being able to reach a unanimous verdict. They were hopelessly deadlocked. The judge then declared a mistrial. Soon after, rumors began to circulate that rather than "doomed," as his attorney had complained, the vote in the jury room had been ten to two for Whitmore's acquittal.

Glass heard about the verdict with a mixture of relief and regret. He'd attended parts of the trial to take notes when Micelli, Ayala and DiPrima testified. DiPrima had confronted him in a hallway outside the courtroom for taking sides against the Brooklyn police. Mel had responded, "You guys brought it on yourself." He believed what he said to the detective, but that didn't mean he welcomed the ramifications.

Although there was no way of quantifying it, the trial seemed to represent a major shift in how the public, as represented by that jury, perceived the NYPD. After Whitmore's arrest in April 1964, the public's perception of New York's finest was at a peak. Thanks to their dedication and skill, the "Brooklyn Psycho" was off the streets and young women were safe from his depredations. They had scoffed at Whitmore's contentions that he'd been beaten and intimidated into confessing to crimes he didn't commit. The police didn't lie; they didn't frame innocent young black men. The detectives had been hailed as heroes. They were lauded in print, on broadcasts and in public award ceremonies.

However, a year later, the attitude had shifted dramatically. The case against Whitmore had been dissected in the press both locally and nationally—called a "frame job" and a "railroading." The young black man was innocent, and the police were the bad guys. It was a shame, Glass had thought as he'd watched the events unfold. While he didn't know it yet, this had helped to light a slow-burning fuse on a powder keg that would explode into a decade of unrest and violence in New York's black community.

All he knew at the time was that the anger expressed toward the NYPD in the Whitmore "snafu" fit the mood of the country. Civil rights marchers were clashing with the police and with white supremacists throughout the South, sometimes with deadly results. Elsewhere protests against the Vietnam War were erupting, including twenty-five thousand who marched on Washington, DC, where—for the first time—speakers referred to "the Establishment" of the government as though speaking about a foreign enemy. It seemed to Glass that the country was being torn apart by mistrust and even justifiable anger about government excesses.

Yet, all of it seemed to fly above the head of the Brooklyn DA, who ignored the pernicious nature of prosecutorial abuse as one of the reasons that in May 1965, the New York State Legislature voted to abolish capital punishment. There was no doubt that they were aware that an innocent man could have been sentenced to death, or as one of the lawmakers told the press, "This is the year of Whitmore."

However, even with a mistrial that had only narrowly missed acquitting Whitmore—by all reports—the Brooklyn DA announced that his office would retry George in the Edmonds case, too. And so, having already spent eighteen months in jail without being convicted of anything, George Whitmore Jr. was sent back behind bars to await his fate.

Although believing it was a travesty of justice that Whitmore remained in jail, Glass knew that the only thing he could do about it was help convict the man who really had killed Janice Wylie and Emily Hoffert. Convicting Richard Robles, while demonstrating that Whitmore's confession was a sham, would be another spotlight turned onto the unfairness of the Brooklyn DAO's position.

* * *

Leaning back a bit in his chair at the prosecution table, Glass glanced over at the three men occupying the defense table. Closest to him was Mack Dollinger, the tall, charming attorney who had also represented Robles back in 1960. He was familiar to the prosecutors because he'd been a former ADA, until leaving the office in the mid-1950s. He was clever, well-trained and pulled out all the stops to defend his client. Assisting Dollinger was Frank Backer, also a seasoned courtroom veteran.

Between the defense attorneys, wearing a gray suit coat, green sweater vest and button-down white shirt, but no tie, Richard Robles sat looking at the jury with no expression on his face. Nine months in the Tombs without heroin had improved the clarity of his eyes and he'd put on some weight, but the junkie pallor had only been traded in for the pasty white skin of jail. Still, they'd cleaned him up, and had given him a shave and a haircut. With his dark, wavy hair, long on top and clipped on the sides, combined with his boyish good looks, he could have passed for an English major at Columbia University. Sitting behind him in the first row behind the defense table were his common-law wife, Dolly Ruiz, and their young daughter.

As he looked at the defendant, in his head Glass could hear Robles's voice from the night of January 26: *"It wasn't panic. Something went wrong."*

"Something went wrong. Something went wrong." That statement had echoed in Glass's mind ever since. Something had indeed gone wrong, and now it was up to the prosecution to set it as right as possible.

"Mr. Keenan, are the People ready with your opening statement?" Judge Davidson inquired.

Keenan rose from his seat. "Yes, Your Honor."

"Then please proceed."

CHAPTER 17

With all eyes fixed on him, John Keenan stood before the jury and opened the trial of Richard Robles with a description of the building at 57 East Eighty-eighth Street, which he noted was "ten stories tall, with four apartments on each floor." While most spectators, including the jurors, may have hardly noticed such a mundane beginning, Mel Glass smiled. Nothing Keenan did was without a reason—even if his motive wasn't clear at the moment.

A product of Jesuit schools, Keenan knew every fact of a case going in and used it to his best advantage. And in this trial, he'd relied on Glass both for his knowledge and his thoughts about how to go about prosecuting this most unusual case. They'd spent hours leading up to the trial discussing strategy, particularly how to combat the defense's main weapon, George Whitmore Jr.'s confession.

Keenan had begun implementing the strategy back during voir dire—the jury selection process that began on October 11. First he'd read the indictment to the prospective jurors, charging Robles with two counts of murder in the first degree: "The defendant in the County of New York, on or about August 28,

1963, willfully, feloniously and of malice aforethought struck and killed Janice Wylie and Emily Hoffert with a knife."

Then he gave a brief introduction of the case, including a small aside belittling the fact that expected "defense witness" George Whitmore Jr. had confessed to two crimes in Brooklyn "and then threw in this one, for good measure." He didn't dwell on the subject long, though; he had to be careful about casting doubt on all confessions as the prosecution case also would be relying on statements Robles made on January 26.

After his description of the building in his opening, Keenan continued to pour the foundation for their plan as he spoke briefly about the three roommates in apartment 3C, and the morning of August 28, 1963. Almost offhandedly, he noted that Katherine Olsen took out the garbage before leaving for work, and "then closed and double-locked the service entrance door."

Keenan then moved swiftly on to what the jurors could expect to learn from the Delaneys, and that they'd hear portions of many hours of tapes from the listening device the couple had consented to have planted in their apartment.

Without dwelling on any one topic, the senior assistant district attorney arrived at January 26, 1965, and the defendant's arrest and his subsequent statements to detectives: "I don't know, Downes. I went to pull a lousy burglary and I wound up killing two girls."

Keenan strode over to the defense table, pointed at Richard Robles and graphically explained, "Simply stated, the People will prove that this defendant annihilated, slaughtered and raped a young, innocent, defenseless woman, Janice Wylie, in her apartment, and then brutally, virtually decapitated her roommate Emily Hoffert. All because he wanted a few bucks to satisfy his drug addiction."

He ended by telling the jury to keep an open mind "until you've heard all of the evidence, because after everything has been presented, I will ask you in the name of the *People of the*

State of New York, and in the interests of justice, to convict the defendant of the murders of Janice Wylie and Emily Hoffert."

After Mack Dollinger waived his right to give an opening statement, John Keenan progressed to laying the bricks of the prosecution strategy with his first witness, John A. Farrell, a civil engineer who'd worked for the DAO since 1950.

Farrell brought two diagrams to the witness stand: one of the apartment, the other of the courtyards and passageways of the 57 East Eighty-eighth Street residence. The latter depicted the service stairwells and the vent shafts that ran up the back of the building between the service stairwell windows and the kitchen windows. He noted that the only entrance to the service stairwells in the lobby was through a lobby door that locked automatically and could only be opened from the stairwell side.

Keenan then moved quickly on to the next witness, Detective Nicholas Perrino, whose primary job was as a crime scene photographer. He identified a series of photographs that he'd taken in and around apartment 3C. Again, the witness described what the jury would see in the photographs—such as the back of the building or the frosted glass windows on the ground floor, which prevented people from seeing inside to the lobby—without any elaboration. However, at this time Keenan held back the photographs of the deceased women for later.

In rapid succession Keenan next called the witnesses who would set the scene for the events leading up to the horrific discovery of the two murder victims, such as Brierly Reybine, the young woman who worked with Janice Wylie at *Newsweek*. Reybine testified that she'd telephoned Janice first that morning, and then later in the afternoon when Janice didn't show up for work.

Then the senior ADA called Katherine Olsen Fagen to the stand. Pale and anxious, Olsen, who had since married and went by the name Fagen, settled onto the witness chair. Keeping her eyes on Keenan, she avoided looking at Robles. With the prosecutor guiding her, she reviewed the events of the morning—the arrival of the towels from Bloomingdale's, the excitement over the March on Washington, the telephone call that Janice picked up, and placing the trash on the service stairwell landing before "locking and bolting the door."

It seemed like such an innocuous statement, yet Glass knew how important it was—not just to the prosecution case, but to Fagen. When he told her after the trial that they now knew beyond a doubt that she'd locked the door that morning, she sighed and then broke down into tears. For two years she'd heard the whispers and read the newspaper stories that implied that she'd left the door open and consequently contributed to the deaths of her roommates.

During witness preparation, Mel tried to encourage her to simply tell the truth and not worry about any other issues. She seemed relieved by his reassurance and sincere concern for her.

However, the relief did not prevent her from crying on the witness stand as she recalled coming home that evening and discovering the ransacked bedrooms, the bloody knife in the bathroom and the open kitchen stairwell door.

"Could you please tell us where in your apartment you kept your spoons, forks and knives?" Keenan asked.

"In the kitchen," Fagen replied.

"Could you tell us precisely where?"

"We kept them in a drawer under the counter."

"One last question in this area, Mrs. Fagen, was there a table in the kitchen?"

Fagen shook her head. "No, there was no table in the kitchen. It was too small a room."

Without comment and matter-of-factly, Keenan moved on to the rest of her testimony. She recalled how she'd been asked to accompany a detective to the room where her friends lay butchered. Through tears and sobs, she recalled the horror of what she'd seen.

"Mrs. Fagen," Keenan said gently, "did you ever speak to any detectives with the last names Bulger, Ayala or DiPrima?"

The young woman frowned as she dabbed at her eyes and nose. "I don't believe so," she said. "I don't recall talking to anyone with those names."

If anyone in the courtroom thought Keenan might give some clue as to why he had asked her about the Brooklyn detectives, they were going to have to wait.

After Katherine Fagen's brief cross-examination, she stepped down. Judge Davidson told Keenan to call his next witness.

"The People call Mr. Max Wylie."

A hush fell over the courtroom as a frail, white-haired man, bent over as though under a great weight, entered the courtroom through a side door leading from the witness room. He blinked several times as if he hadn't expected such a large crowd, all of whom were staring at him. But he spotted John Keenan, who smiled reassuringly and gestured toward the witness stand; gathering himself, he walked haltingly past the first row of spectators into the well of the court and was led to the witness chair by the court clerk.

After Wylie was sworn in and took his seat, Keenan began his examination with a series of straightforward questions about his family life and work. From his answers the jurors learned that he and his wife, Lambert, had lived on 55 East Eighty-sixth Street for twenty-four years; they were also informed that Janice was born on March 6, 1942, and she had an older sister, Pamela. Wylie was employed by a Madison Avenue advertising firm, and that was where he'd spent August 28, 1963, at his desk, except for a short lunch break.

In fact, he'd been at his desk late that afternoon when he received a call from his worried wife. Janice had not shown up at work, and no one seemed to be able to reach her or knew her whereabouts. He'd gone home; and then after Kate Olsen called to say the apartment had been ransacked, he and his wife had hurried over to 57 East Eighty-eighth Street.

Stopping often to catch his breath and regroup, Max Wylie grieved as he relived the nightmare. Upon arriving at the apartment, he told his wife and Kate to remain in the living room; then he ventured down the hallway and looked into the first bedroom, "which was in a frightful disarray." When he saw the bloody knife in the bathroom, then dreading each step, he walked down the hallway to the second bedroom, where he nudged the door open with his foot. Frightened by the room's chaotic state and the blood-covered bed, he'd forced himself farther in, until he saw the bodies.

"They were both close together," he testified, his voice on the verge of cracking, the tears rolling down his cheeks. "The space was very confining. The body of Emily was dressed. The body of Janice was nude."

Then he spotted a blue wool blanket at Emily's feet. "When I saw the mutilation of the girls, I feared it might be proper police procedure for them to ask Mrs. Wylie to see what I saw, and I pulled the blanket over both the girls' bodies, covering them as much as I could."

Only now did Keenan hand Max Wylie two photographs—People's Exhibits 29 and 30.

Although he'd seen them before—indeed, he couldn't get those images out of his mind—Max Wylie looked like he'd been struck in the chest with a sledgehammer.

"Do these photographs fairly and accurately depict the scene in the bedroom inside apartment 3C that night?" Keenan asked.

Wylie nodded and tried to speak, but his voice at first came out as just a strangled cry. He took a deep breath and tried again. In a hushed tone, he answered, "Yes, that is what I saw."

A few minutes later, Keenan wrapped up his examination of

the witness. Notwithstanding all the cases he had tried, it was always painful—and in this case gut-wrenching—to have to call a member of the deceased's family to the stand. Particularly a mother or a father. But it was necessary because in every murder case, the prosecution had to prove two things: The deceased was, in fact, dead, and had died as a result of the criminal acts of the defendant. In order to satisfy the first criterion—even though in most homicide cases, and this one in particular, it was not an issue—the deceased, nevertheless, had to be identified by the family member, which usually happened when that individual was called to the morgue.

When Wylie was finally excused from the witness stand, Mel Glass stood up and then accompanied him back to the witness room. The grieving father looked at the young assistant district attorney. Wylie's eyes were welling with tears that he no longer fought to hold back.

"How'd I do?" he asked, and broke into sobs.

Stepping forward, Mel put his arm around the other man's shoulders. "You did fine, Max," he said softly. "You did just fine."

CHAPTER 18

"He showed up at my pad a little before noon and said he was in trouble—that he'd just killed two girls."

As he testified from the witness stand, Nathan "Jimmy" Delaney scratched the stubble on his chin and tugged at the unaccustomed tie around his neck. He glanced over at the defense table, where Richard Robles sat impassively staring back at him.

Delaney shook his head—whether that was out of sorrow or disgust, it was impossible to tell. The defendant, however, showed no emotion as he turned to look at the jurors.

Watching the exchange between the two former friends, Glass recalled the evening just slightly more than a year before when he first heard the Delaneys talk about the morning a blood-stained Ricky Robles came to their apartment. That had been followed by the confrontation in his office between the couple and the defendant. All of it set into motion a chain of events that culminated in Delaney's appearance on the witness stand.

Prior to Jimmy Delaney taking the stand that day, Detective John Lynch had been called to describe what he saw and what he did when he arrived the evening of August 28, 1963, at apartment 3C. As he walked the jurors through the apartment and into the bloodstained bedroom, the detective answered several seemingly innocuous questions from John Keenan, though Glass knew they were anything but throwaways.

Keenan made sure that the witness described the kitchen in detail: the open window, the open door "with no sign of forced entry," the open drawer beneath the counter that contained forks, spoons and knives, the six-pack Pepsi container, with two bottles missing, the absence of a kitchen table. Similar attention was paid to the detective's recollection of the stairwell door that opened into the lobby: that there was no sign on the lobby side denoting where the door led, or if it was an exit; that it shut and locked itself automatically; and once shut, it could only be opened without a key from the stairwell side.

"It couldn't be opened from the lobby," the detective added.

As Lynch discussed the condition of the murder room and the victims, Keenan asked him about the bloody eyeglasses on the bed and a jar of Noxzema lying on the ground. Then he inquired whether Lynch had seen a clock radio.

"Yes," the detective replied, "it was stopped at ten thirty-seven A.M."

When Lynch remarked that he'd seen a razor blade on the floor of the death room, Keenan asked him to describe the blade.

"It had arrows stamped on the side, indicating it came from a dispenser," Lynch replied.

"Did you see a paper wrapper for a razor blade on the bathroom floor?"

Lynch frowned and shook his head. "No, there was no paper wrapper. Again, the blade was the sort you get out of a dispenser, not a wrapper."

Under cross-examination Mack Dollinger questioned Detective Lynch about taking the photograph that was found on George Whitmore Jr. to Max Wylie and others in the early-morning hours after Whitmore's arrest. The detective agreed that Wylie denied the blonde in the photograph was Janice, and that he'd informed Captain Frank Weldon and Detective Edward Bulger of that fact.

As Glass listened, he knew this was the first glimpse into the defense scheme: The police knew right away that Whitmore had lied about the photograph. They couldn't convict him, so they had to set up the defendant as a stand-in.

Glass shook his head in disgust, knowing what was to come, because he had informed Mack Dollinger about the lack of identification on the photograph.

When Detective Lynch stepped down, Keenan continued by calling associate medical examiner (ME) Dr. Bela Dur and the renowned chief ME, Dr. Milton Helpern. One at a time, they testified regarding the cause of death of each of the girls, describing in explicit detail the number and type of wounds.

Lost, perhaps, in the horrific account of the autopsies were two notations that Helpern, a white-haired grandfatherly type, made about Janice Wylie. In one observation he stated that Noxzema had been smeared on Janice's genital and anal areas. In the other notation, he said that when the young woman was disemboweled, the killer had punctured her intestines three times, releasing digestive gases that would have caused a foul odor.

Glass watched the jurors' faces grimace at the chief medical examiner's remark, maybe wondering if such disturbing minutia was really necessary. But he knew when Jimmy Delaney was called to the stand that the stage was set. Every issue he and Keenan had discussed in their strategy sessions, every witness, diagram and photograph—no matter how ostensibly mundane—brought before the jury were metaphorically tiles in a mosaic. Each one was not of immediate evidentiary impact; but when put together in a finished picture, they would point inexorably to the defendant's guilt.

* * *

However, that was not readily apparent when thirty-six-year-old Jimmy Delaney began his testimony by answering questions about his personal background. Although he'd been a U.S. Marine, the witness admitted he'd been addicted to heroin since 1954 and had a long criminal history, which began in 1948 with a conviction for attempted robbery. Most of his other convictions were for minor drug possession and sales, but he'd spent most of his adult life in and out of jails and prisons, including thirty months in a federal penitentiary for the sale of narcotics.

With the biographic account out of the way, the real questioning began: "Could you tell the jury, please, if you saw the defendant on August 28, 1963?" Keenan asked.

"Yeah," Delaney answered, turning to look at Robles. "He showed up at my pad a little before noon and said he was in trouble—that he'd just killed two girls."

At first, Delaney testified, he was worried that Robles might have led the police to his apartment. His friend assured him, however, that he'd taken precautions. After fleeing from the murder scene, Robles said he'd taken a taxi downtown, got out, walked some distance and then caught another taxi back uptown to the West Side, and then another cab cross town to Delaney's apartment. All of this just in case the first taxi driver recalled picking up a possible suspect near the scene of a double murder.

Robles was carrying a paper bag when he arrived at the apartment. It contained a green sports shirt with blood on it and a pair of pink rubber gloves. He also had a bloodstain on his left pant leg. More blood had soaked through to the white T-shirt he was wearing beneath a jacket, the killer said, he had gotten from his victims' apartment.

"He wanted a change of clothing, so I gave him pants and a shirt," Delaney told the jurors.

The defendant had also wanted heroin and handed over some cash that he claimed he got from the purse of one of the victims.

Leaving his wife behind with Robles, the witness said, he was gone about forty-five minutes before returning with the drugs.

When he got back to the apartment, Robles and his wife were talking about the murders. "He said he made one of them give him a blow job."

The three addicts shot up the heroin, after which the defendant left the apartment. But he'd returned about ten that night with the clothes he'd borrowed and a newspaper that already had a story about the murder of the two young women who'd been stabbed to death in their Upper East Side apartment. "He said those were the girls he'd been talking about."

The defendant returned again the next day with more newspapers, which now had photographs of the victims. "I asked why he had to kill the girls. . . . One was pretty attractive. He told me that she wasn't as attractive as the newspaper made her out to be."

"Did he tell you how he got into the apartment?" Keenan asked.

"Yeah, he said he got in through the kitchen window," Delaney answered. "He went out a stairwell window and stepped on a vent so he could reach the windowsill and pulled himself up."

At the prosecution table, Glass glanced at the jurors to see how they'd reacted to the answer. He could almost sense their minds collectively recognizing the mosaic falling together: recalling the photographs of the back of the building, Detective Lynch's description of the open kitchen window and Kate Fagen's testimony that she double-locked the service door after she took out the garbage.

John Keenan's examination of the witness wore into the late afternoon and then into the next morning. Delaney testified that Richard Robles told him that as he was sexually assaulting the blonde, the girl with the thick glasses came in. "He told her to take them off, but she wouldn't. She said she wanted to be able to identify him."

The jurors listened raptly as the witness recalled Robles's description of his actions after he decided that the women had to die: striking them on the head with the Pepsi bottles, the frenzy of slashing and stabbing that followed.

"One of the girls took a long time to die. He said he had to stab her several times up through her stomach to get to her heart."

Glass knew there wasn't a juror who wasn't thinking of Dr. Helpern's testimony regarding the odor emitted when Delaney added, "Robles said the smell was awful—so bad he almost threw up."

Covered with blood and gore, the killer had then gone into the bathroom, where he took a shower and cleaned the knife, which he left on the sink, Delaney testified Robles had told him and Margie.

As the defense would have certainly raised the issue if Keenan had not, the prosecutor asked what had brought Delaney to the attention of the police in the Wylie-Hoffert murders.

"I killed a drug pusher named Cruz," Delaney admitted. "It was self-defense. He hit me with a steel rod."

CHAPTER 19

Mel Glass looked over at the defense table as the court clerk handed the jury foreman a sheaf of printouts as he instructed the jurors to take one and pass the others to their peers. Mack Dollinger kept a small smile plastered on his face as he watched the jurors, while Richard Robles sat with his head bowed, staring blankly at the table in front of him. In a few moments, the jurors would hear him talk about the murders in his own words as they read along on the transcripts they'd just been given.

It was November 3, a Wednesday afternoon, five days since Jimmy Delaney last took the stand. After John Keenan finished his direct examination of Delaney, Dollinger had jumped to his feet as though answering the bell in a boxing ring. The thrust of his cross-examination was primarily focused on the promises the prosecution had made regarding the dismissal of the Cruz homicide, Delaney's criminal history and portraying him as a drug-addicted killer desperate to make a deal.

Through his questioning, Dollinger also implied that Delaney knew that if his story was believed, he would be eligible for the $10,000 reward offered by *Newsweek* for the arrest and conviction of the killer. Delaney contended he didn't know about the reward until just before the trial, but the defense attorney merely scoffed at his answer.

Glass thought Delaney had held up well during a day and a half on the stand. He'd looked forward to Margie's testimony, which was supposed to follow immediately. However, she'd had a miscarriage while her husband was on the stand, and they'd had to postpone her appearance for a few days.

Scrambling to fill the time, John Keenan and Mel Glass decided to introduce the tape recordings of the conversations that had occurred among Jimmy and Margie Delaney and Richard Robles. So the day after Jimmy's testimony ended, the jury was excused so that the defense attorneys could occupy an office in the DAO to listen to the parts of three separate conversations that the prosecutors wanted to play in the courtroom.

To accommodate the audio presentation, the courtroom had been set up as a virtual sound studio. There was a speaker for the judge, the defense and prosecution, and two speakers for the jury. One of the detectives who'd assisted in preparing the recorded conversations sat next to the machine. He was ready to turn it on and off so that the jury would only hear those portions approved by Judge Davidson. It would take split-second timing. If he waited too long and the jurors heard something they weren't supposed to hear, it could result in a mistrial; if he turned it off too quickly, they'd miss important passages.

Against Mack Dollinger's objections, the prosecutors also had the recordings transcribed so that the jury could follow along more easily. All three conversations that were prepared for the jurors had occurred in the Delaney apartment in January '65 after the better recording equipment was installed. Glass played them for ADA Vince Dermody, the senior member of the Homicide Bureau, who was revered by those participants, commentators and observers of the New York justice system to be without equal. His trial experience and sound judgment set him apart; he was the lead knight at Hogan's Round Table. And when he heard the tapes, he was extremely pleased that the recordings established unequivocally the evidentiary corroboration that was required to proceed against the defendant and would be able to dismiss with respect to Whitmore.

Judge Davidson informed the jurors that the transcripts were aids to help them follow along while listening to the recordings. "But the real evidence is the tape. What you hear, not what you read, is what's important here."

With that, Judge Davidson nodded to John Keenan, who informed the jury that the three excerpted conversations they were about to hear revealed in substance that the defendant, Richard Robles, "in his own words voluntarily incriminated himself." He began by playing the first taped conversation, in which Robles talked about how he "eventually" got the glasses off Emily Hoffert, that he was "crazy when I killed that girl" and his circuitous taxi journeys after fleeing the murder scene.

In the second tape, Robles told the Delaneys, "If I could just plant in my mind that you made it all up, I would take the lie detector test."

As that conversation was played, Mel Glass thought about how Robles, instead of taking the test, tried to commit suicide by overdosing. *Because he knew he couldn't pass the test.*

Finally John Keenan introduced the third conversation between Robles and Jimmy Delaney. "In this conversation the defendant is reading a newspaper," he said, pausing for a moment before adding, "I would like to apologize in advance for what you are about to hear, which is graphic in nature, but we believe it is important." Keenan nodded to the detective, who switched on the machine for the third time:

Robles: It says I forced Janice into an act of perversion. That's
supposed to mean she sucked my dick.
Delaney: You sucked her dick?
Robles: No, she sucked my dick.

Glass noted the sudden blushes, grimaces and scowls on the faces of the jurors. The language had come as a shock, but he was sure that they would also recognize what it meant: Robles had just admitted that he'd sexually assaulted Janice Wylie.

When the machine was turned off, Keenan again apologized for the language. And that, he added, concluded the People's presentation of the recorded conversations.

The next day Margie Delaney was called to the stand and entered the courtroom. She looked frail and haggard, far beyond her thirty years. Still, when she took her seat, she glared at Robles before turning to face John Keenan.

As he had with her husband, Keenan started with her personal history. She said she'd been married to Jimmy for twelve years and had three kids, ages eight to twelve, Francisco, Nathan and Rebecca. She'd been convicted twice on narcotics charges; the first conviction had been suspended and she'd been placed on probation for the other.

She again glared at Robles, who kept his eyes on the jury, when she identified him as the common-law husband of her aunt Dolly Ruiz. Margie said she'd known him since 1956.

Like her husband before her, Margie recalled the day Robles showed up at her home. He was carrying a paper bag and had blood on his shirt and pants. "I'd just gone into the kitchen to make some coffee when I heard the door buzzer," she said. "So I was in the other room when Jimmy let him in. But I heard him say that he was in trouble because he'd killed two women." There was further conversation.

Jimmy left to buy some dope. Robles then told her more

about the killings. "He said he hit them with Pepsi bottles to try to knock them out. One of them was unconscious right away, but the other one fought back. He said he cut her throat on one of the beds to stop her from screaming."

The killer told her that the second girl was lying between the bed and the window when he finished her off. "She was unconscious, but he said she wouldn't die, so he kept stabbing her in the heart."

Robles had shown her a pair of pink rubber gloves, which he took out of the paper bag. He'd even pulled them on and pressed his fingers against a mirror to make sure they didn't leave fingerprints.

There was no particular reason he'd chosen that building or apartment other than the open window had presented the opportunity, Margie said. He'd only wanted money to buy drugs.

The young killer had told her that he'd struggled with one of the girls to remove her glasses. Then he'd tied them back to back on the bed while he thought for several minutes about what to do next. "He decided he needed to kill them and told me he said, 'God forgive me,' and then went to the kitchen to get Pepsi bottles. He thought it would be less painful if he knocked them out first."

On cross-examination Mack Dollinger had stuck with his strategy of portraying Margie Delaney as a drug addict who was trying to help her husband get out of a murder rap.

"Would you lie for your husband?" the defense attorney asked.

"Yes," Margie replied, "but I'm not lying now."

As the tiny woman climbed down from the witness stand, she looked at Mel Glass, who nodded solemnly. He was recalling that evening in October 1964 when she told him her story. He knew at that moment that he was hearing the truth.

As he'd told Paddy Lappin and Thomas Cavanaugh outside his office in the hallway that night, he knew it was the truth because the details of what she said matched the evidence. There were some important details that were not memorialized in any police reports, including the DD5s.

"We know that both women were struck with Pepsi bottles," he'd said, "and that Janice's skull was fractured, but Emily's was not. And according to the medical examiner's report, Emily had her throat cut on the bed—the blood on the mattress was type A, the same as Emily's. Most of the blood on the floor was type O. Janice had type O blood. The ME also noted that Janice was stabbed five or six times in and around her heart. Only the real killer could have told her that—only the real killer could have known. And nowhere in the file—not in one of the more than a thousand police reports—will you find mention that the bedroom had an awful odor."

CHAPTER 20

As Detective David Downes followed Margie Delaney to the stand, Mel Glass reflected on all the careful groundwork and trial preparation he and John Keenan had taken to reach the last few witnesses. And how it was all about to pay off.

The focus of the mosaic was more sharply defined on January 26, 1965, when Richard Robles confessed to Glass that "something went wrong," but he wanted to speak to his attorney, Mack Dollinger, before he would tell the whole story. It might have ended there, with the defense attorney refusing to let him speak anymore. Yet, the suspect—tormented in his own mind by his evil deeds—had not waited.

As Detective Downes now told the jury, he had arrived at the Twenty-third Precinct that evening at Glass's direction and eventually had a conversation with the accused: "I don't know, Downes. I went to pull a lousy burglary and I wound up killing two girls," Robles stated.

The young murderer had gone on to tell him the story of that day: He got into the apartment by climbing in the kitchen window. He'd forced the first girl to perform oral sex. He'd struck both women with Pepsi bottles. He broke the blade of one of the knives when he stabbed Emily in the back. He'd left the apartment through the kitchen service stairwell door. He took a cab to the Delaneys' apartment. He'd thrown his bloodstained shirt in the East River.

Downes went on to testify, "I asked Robles, 'So are the Delaneys telling the truth?' He said yes."

As the detective stepped down from the stand, Downes and Glass exchanged a meaningful look. On that evening in January, the detective had decided he wouldn't tell anyone about the confession because he didn't think anyone would believe him. It would have been just his word against Robles's.

However, Lieutenant Thomas Cavanaugh had then entered the room, and Detective Downes had suggested that Robles repeat his story. The young man complied, as the lieutenant told the jury after following Downes to the stand.

They'd been joined by two more detectives, who also had heard his confession. One of them asked Robles what he felt when he heard that George Whitmore Jr. had been arrested for the murders in Brooklyn.

"Relieved," Robles responded.

Another asked if he wanted the detective to say anything to his mother and Dolly Ruiz.

"Ask them to forgive me." And then Richard Robles began to cry.

CHAPTER 21

The young black man with the acne-scarred face stared sullenly down at the defense attorney, who was approaching the witness stand like a lion stalking an antelope. Mack Dollinger obviously believed that George Whitmore Jr. would crumble under questioning, as he had with the Brooklyn detectives.

Despite the judge's admonition to the jury that Whitmore wasn't on trial in this case, that hoped-for misperception was essentially a large part of Dollinger's strategy. If he could make a case to the jury that Whitmore was the real killer or, barring that, show that he was at least as good a suspect as Robles, the defense attorney might sow enough doubt to win an acquittal. However, the witness, dressed in a gray jail jumpsuit, was getting to be an old hand at testifying. He had grown tired of being pushed around.

Whitmore was now twenty-one. As he'd told the press, which had gone from labeling him the "Brooklyn Psycho" to championing his cause, he was living a nightmare that seemed to have no end—especially as he was still under indictment for the Edmonds and Estrada cases in Brooklyn.

* * *

The first witness called by the defense had been Liam Gynt, who'd been working as the doorman at the 57 East Eighty-eighth residence on the day of the murders. The thirty-seven-year-old was married, with five kids, but he was a "real lush" in Mel Glass's opinion. Gynt's memory and judgment had been clouded by alcohol.

In fact, the defense owed it to Glass that the doorman was even present in the courtroom. First, during the course of the investigation, Glass had interviewed Gynt, who gave conflicting versions on what he saw and heard that day. So Glass turned him and the questionable information over to the defense.

Thereafter, the defense advised Glass that they wanted to speak to Gynt and possibly call him as a witness at trial. When Glass called him before the trial and told him about the defense's intentions, Gynt, who was a merchant marine, gave the impression that he was going to "ship out" before he could be served with a subpoena. So Glass called Dollinger's office and said that if they wanted Gynt, they had better serve him immediately.

On the witness stand, Gynt recounted how he'd delivered a package to apartment 3C from Bloomingdale's and was met at the door by the then-unmarried Kate Olsen. Charged with picking up the garbage twice a day from the stairwell landings, he said that when he picked up the garbage between ten and eleven that morning, he hadn't heard anything from apartment 3C. However, when he returned at about three in the afternoon, and was, in fact, in the hall across from 3C, he heard someone moving around in the apartment and the sound of water running. He also testified that he'd seen the service stairwell door ajar at the same time.

After getting off work at four o'clock, Gynt said, he'd gone around the corner to a bar, where he drank until about ten that night. When he went home, he learned that the police wanted to talk to him.

Of course, Mack Dollinger's point in putting Gynt on the stand was the witness claiming to have heard someone in the apartment—presumably the "real" killer—running the water in the afternoon. The Delaneys, however, had testified that Robles arrived at their apartment before noon, claiming that's when he confessed to killing two women in the morning.

When Glass and Keenan discussed Gynt's potential testimony the night before, they didn't think that Liam Gynt was purposefully trying to throw water on the prosecution case against Robles. However, given that Glass and Keenan felt Gynt was an unreliable witness—and that two years had passed—they believed he may have "compressed time" and had mixed up what he saw, heard and when.

On cross-examination Keenan asked, "Don't you remember telling Mr. Glass that the door to 3C was closed in the afternoon?"

"Then I made a mistake," Gynt said. "'Cause I know the door, like I say, was ajar. It wasn't locked. In other words, you could have pushed the door in and walked right in."

"Mr. Gynt, isn't it a fact that you told Detective Zinkand the next day, August 29 of 1963, that the kitchen door was closed about three o'clock when you were picking up the garbage?"

Gynt furrowed his brow. "Maybe I did. Maybe I didn't. I don't remember."

After Liam Gynt stepped down, Mack Dollinger called George Whitmore Jr. to the stand. As he took a seat, Whitmore glanced briefly over at his mother, who sat in the seat behind the prosecution table.

Glass had turned to follow the witness's look. His gaze met that of Bernadine Whitmore, who gave him a slight smile and a nod. Her son was still a prisoner, but she knew that Mel Glass and the New York DAO, which had formally dismissed the indictment against George, had done what they could to correct an injustice. She had called Mel shortly before the Robles trial to thank him for his efforts.

"You told me you would find the truth," she said. "And you lived up to your promise."

While on the stand, Whitmore was wearing a pair of thick, black-rimmed eyeglasses, which he needed to see the documents that Mack Dollinger gave to him, one at a time, as he started his questioning. The first documents were Detective Edward Bulger's notes from his interrogation.

Looking carefully over the pages, Whitmore then handed them back, saying the signature on the pages wasn't his. Presented next with a diagram of the East Eighty-eighth Street apartment, Whitmore also denied drawing it, as Bulger had claimed. It was an important point, as the alleged suspect's "knowledge" of the apartment layout was one of Bulger's contentions that proved Whitmore had been there. But now the witness said all he had done was place marks on the diagram, which had already been drawn, under the guidance of the detectives in the room.

When Dollinger tried to get him to admit that he'd confessed to going to the East Eighty-eighth Street apartment, Whitmore said it was a lie. He'd been at his parents' house in Wildwood on the morning of August 28, 1963; and then in the afternoon, he'd walked to the Ivy Hotel, where he later met Ludie Montgomery.

If Mack Dollinger thought he was going to be able to cow George Whitmore Jr. as the detectives had, he was mistaken. Whitmore repeatedly denied being in the apartment or murdering two young women—no matter how many times the defense lawyer asked, or rephrased, the question. He said everything he'd confessed to in Brooklyn had been suggested to him by the police.

"I told them I wasn't in the building," he testified. "But they insisted that when I went into the building and pushed open the door, the first thing I was supposed to have saw was soda bottles. Everything was suggested to me this way."

Sometimes he made up answers he thought the detectives wanted to hear, Whitmore said, and made sense according to the story they fed him. An example was when he told the detectives that after the killings, he'd traveled back to his uncle's house in Brooklyn, where he found the older man sitting on the doorstep and asked him for a dollar to buy a hot dog.

Finally, unable to get Whitmore to budge on his denials, Dollinger turned him over to Keenan for cross-examination.

The prosecutor started by getting George Whitmore Jr. to discuss his impoverished background and that he had been eighteen years old when he completed the eighth grade and then dropped out of school.

Under John Keenan's questioning, Whitmore noted that he didn't have his eyeglasses—they'd been lost—when he was arrested in Brooklyn. Nearly blind without them, he'd been unable to read any notes or clearly see the diagram. They'd asked him a lot of questions about a photograph he'd been carrying in his wallet, but they wouldn't believe him when he told them where he got it.

"I told the police that I got the photograph while I was at the dump," he testified. "One of the detectives told me that this picture looked like a girl they knew. They insisted that I got this picture from an apartment on Eighty-eighth Street. I told them the picture did not come from Eighty-eighth Street and that I never been there."

"So the detectives kept telling you that it came from an apartment on Eighty-eighth Street?" Keenan repeated for emphasis.

"Yes, sir. But I never been to Eighty-eighth Street in my life."

Keenan used the moment to ask Whitmore if he could describe how to get from Brooklyn to Manhattan. When they were discussing trial strategy, Glass had told him about his meeting with Bernadine Whitmore, who'd said her son would have no idea how to get around in New York City.

On the witness stand, Whitmore furrowed his brow as though trying his best to see if he could correctly answer the prosecutor's question. But then he gave up and shook his head. "I don't know, sir," he replied. "I never been out that way by myself."

Keenan then asked if the Brooklyn detectives had said anything to him about the girls he was alleged to have attacked in the East Eighty-eighth Street apartment.

"One of the detectives came in and told me that he had called the girls up and they were all right," Whitmore answered. "One of the detectives said I was supposed to have cut the girls and they went to a hospital, but they were all right. The other detective left the room and was gone maybe five or ten minutes. When he came back, he said he'd spoke to the girls a couple of minutes ago and they was all right."

Keenan next introduced People's Exhibit 72, the photograph of Abbe Mills and Jennifer Holley at Belleplain State Forest. Whitmore readily identified it as the photograph he picked up in the dump. He said Louise Orr was a family friend who sometimes came over to his parents' house for dinner. Blushing, he admitted that he'd written the dedication, *To George From Louise*, on the back of the photograph because he wanted his friends to believe that one of the young women in the photograph was his girlfriend.

As the young man waited for the next question, Mel Glass wondered if George Whitmore Jr. truly understood how much trouble picking up a discarded photograph had cost him, as well as the difficulty it presented to the prosecution of the defendant, Robles. Without it, Detective Edward Bulger would have never questioned him for the Wylie-Hoffert murders.

Then again, if Glass had not pursued locating the young women in the photograph—proving that George's confession to the murders was false—there may have been no reason to question whether his confessions to Edmonds and Estrada were also not true. Glass found it terribly ironic that this one piece of crucial evidence—the photograph, People's Exhibit 72, which had been used to implicate Whitmore initially, because Bulger believed it depicted Janice Wylie—was now the same piece of evidence that exonerated him.

Also, if Glass had not spoken to Bernadine Whitmore, there would have been no alibi witnesses for George Whitmore Jr.

"Mr. Whitmore, do you know a young lady by the name of Ludie Montgomery?" Keenan asked.

"Yes, sir."

"And did you see her at all on August 28, 1963?"

"Yes, sir."

"When did you see her, and where did you see her?"

"This was when I went to the bar, to the Ivy Hotel, to the barroom."

"Were you with her that day?"

"Yes."

At last, George Whitmore Jr. was excused as a witness. As the young man walked between the prosecution and defense tables, heading back to his prison cell, Mel Glass recalled an article that had appeared over the summer in the *New York Journal-American*. Incidentally, this was the same publication that had praised the Brooklyn detectives and had given Bulger its public service award.

In a published interview with Whitmore, the prisoner had reflected on the long interrogation that had led to his arrest: *"I kept saying to myself: When is it all going to end? Why don't they leave me alone? And when they tell me how I was supposed to have done these things, I felt like dirt. I felt so low. In my mind, I kept calling on God, but it seemed like He didn't hear me."*

CHAPTER 22

As the trial of Ricky Robles entered the fourth week of testimony, it was becoming increasingly clear to knowledgeable spectators how unique the proceedings were in the annals of the New York DAO. Here was a prosecution team having to admit that their vaunted Homicide Bureau had made a grievous mistake in indicting George Whitmore Jr., and then ask the jurors to look at the evidence and believe that the prosecutors now had the right man, Richard Robles. And here was the defense out to show that Robles was no better a suspect than Whitmore had been and, in a strange twist, that the New York DAO didn't make mistakes.

Perhaps the most singular irony was the role reversal between the two sides when Mack Dollinger began calling to the stand the Brooklyn detectives and brass involved in the interrogation and arrest of George Whitmore Jr. Now it was the defense attorney's mission to convince the jury of the professionalism, dedication and abilities of men he traditionally would have been at odds with in a trial. On the other hand, it was John Keenan's quest, however reluctantly, to destroy the Brooklyn cops' credibility, competency and, in a couple of instances, call into question their integrity.

The fact that the Brooklyn detectives, particularly Joseph DiPrima and Edward Bulger, had forced the "strange bedfellows" scenario angered and saddened Mel Glass. As Frank Hogan had noted back in January when discussing the ramifications of indicting Robles and dismissing the case against Whitmore, the effects of the mistake on the justice system might be felt for years. He had predicted that in future cases in which the prosecution relied in part or whole on a confession, it would be commonplace for defense attorneys to point to George Whitmore Jr. and argue to juries that if the police could manufacture a false confession in one case, they could manufacture them in all. And that even such a renowned DAO as New York's sometimes indicted innocent people.

Also, by its nature, the trial threatened to create a rift between the DAO and the NYPD, which in normal circumstances were natural allies in the fight to protect citizens, get criminals off the streets and administer justice. But now, John Keenan had to demonstrate to the jury that Brooklyn detectives had not just been sloppy. Rather, they had lied and cheated to frame an innocent man—a position that would be repeated in the newspapers, as well as around the coffeepot in squad rooms. The detectives who'd worked with Mel Glass knew and respected the way he'd gone about his investigation—and that he was right about George Whitmore Jr. and Richard Robles. But the NYPD had thousands of officers, detectives and brass—many of whom didn't know the truth or want to believe that their fellow officers would have framed an innocent person.

That night before, Glass and Keenan had talked about how to avoid painting all members of the NYPD with the same broad brush. Keenan would need to tread lightly while separating cops' natural inclination to protect their own from what they knew, in this case, to be right. It would mean asking them to cross the thin blue line to tell the truth—and even under oath, some would, and some wouldn't.

The effort began with Mack Dollinger's first police witness, Deputy Chief Inspector Edward Carey, assigned to the Brooklyn North Homicide Squad at the time of Whitmore's arrest, but now retired. Carey told the jury that he'd been present during some of the interrogation and that Whitmore appeared relaxed and was answering questions voluntarily.

On cross-examination Keenan showed Carey the photograph of Abbe Mills and Jennifer Holley, People's Exhibit 72, and asked if Detective Bulger had told him he thought the blonde was Janice Wylie.

"We were trying to ID who the girl was," Carey said; then he shrugged. "No one said it was the Wylie girl, because no one knew the Wylie girl."

Keenan wasn't buying it. "Did Bulger tell you that one of the women in the photograph strongly resembled the Wylie girl?"

"He said she was blonde. . . ."

Moving toward the witness, Keenan deliberately and forcefully asked again, "Did Bulger tell you that one of the women in the photograph strongly resembled the Wylie girl?"

Challenged, Carey thought about it for a moment and nervously licked his lips. Then he nodded. "That's right. He did."

As Deputy Chief Inspector Carey was excused, Mack Dollinger rose and announced, "The defense calls Joseph DiPrima."

The barrel-chested detective walked into the courtroom a moment later and looked over the people waiting there as if scanning the crowd for a suspect. When his gaze reached Mel Glass, DiPrima's eyes hardened briefly before he composed himself and strode purposefully to the witness stand to be sworn in.

Another quick glare from the detective as he took his seat reminded Glass of their "whose team are you on" confrontation at the Edmonds trial in April. But the detective's square-jawed face was impassive beneath his salt-and-pepper crew cut as he faced the jury and waited for Dollinger to ask his first question.

Glass wondered if the detective felt compromised as a defense witness after twenty-eight years with the NYPD and currently a detective first grade.

"The highest level of detective—is that right?" Dollinger asked effusively.

"Yes," DiPrima answered without emotion.

After establishing the detective's credentials, Dollinger had him describe the events regarding George Whitmore Jr. from the point when Detective Edward Bulger had poked his head in the door and asked if he could question the suspect. DiPrima gave a general chronology of the interrogation process. He emphatically testified that Whitmore had *not* been intimidated into making his statements and that he'd *not* been fed details of the crime. And, yes, Whitmore had willingly signed the statement written out for him by Bulger.

"Did you or anyone else suggest to Mr. Whitmore that Janice Wylie and Emily Hoffert were okay, still alive?" Dollinger asked.

"I never told George Whitmore the girls were still alive," the detective replied tersely. "And I never heard anyone else say that, too."

Walked right into it, Glass thought as Keenan rose to cross-examine the witness.

Striding right up to the jury box, John Keenan placed a transcript with several pages of notes on the ledge that protruded from the box. He turned and addressed the detective. "Didn't you tell Assistant DA James Hosty, when he arrived at the Seventy-third Precinct, that as far as George Whitmore knew, the girls were still alive? Didn't you tell that to Hosty?"

"Yes, that's correct," DiPrima admitted with a frown.

Keenan was a master chess player in the courtroom and believed it was essential to establish basic fundamental truths as a foundation before moving to checkmate.

"Detective Bulger told you that one of the girls in the photo looked like Janice Wylie. Is that correct?" he asked.

"Yeah," DiPrima conceded, "and I believed him, because he'd been assigned to the Wylie-Hoffert case."

Keenan swiftly changed tactics and moved quickly toward checkmate. "Did you tell Mel Glass in the summer of 1964 that you'd been in the building at 57 East Eighty-eighth Street prior to April 24, 1964, when George Whitmore was arrested? That you'd visited a doctor's office there two or three times?"

DiPrima shot another hard glance at Glass before answering, "Yeah."

"And did you tell Mr. Glass that your doctor told you about the Wylie-Hoffert murders that happened in that building?"

"Yeah, he said that two girls were killed in the building."

"So you knew that the girls were killed in the building at 57 East Eighty-eighth Street *before*," Keenan emphasized and repeated, "*before* George Whitmore was questioned on April 24, 1964?"

DiPrima scowled. "Yeah, I knew it."

"Didn't you testify in Supreme Court in Kings County, Brooklyn, on March sixth of this year, that you had *no* idea that Janice Wylie and Emily Hoffert were murdered in an apartment on East Eighty-eighth Street in Manhattan?"

DiPrima suddenly had the look of a man who realized he'd walked into quicksand with no apparent way out. "I don't remember," he muttered.

Expecting the evasive prevarication, Keenan produced from his papers on the jury box ledge a New York State trial transcript from the Brooklyn proceedings he'd just mentioned. He asked the court to take judicial notice of the official certified copy and enter it into evidence. Judge Davidson so ruled without objection.

With the court's permission, Keenan then handed one set of the pages to DiPrima and kept another for himself. He had already provided the defense with its copy. "Detective, this is from your sworn testimony starting at page seven hundred twenty-eight of the trial transcript. I'll read the questions and you read how you answered for the jury, please."

DiPrima swallowed hard, but he didn't reply.

Keenan began. "'Question—Did George Whitmore mention to you the Eighty-eighth Street apartment and that he got the picture from there before you mentioned anything to him about an Eighty-eighth Street apartment?'"

The detective cleared his throat. "'Answer—I had no idea about . . .'" DiPrima hesitated, understanding now just how fast he was sinking into the bottomless pit.

"Please continue," Keenan insisted.

"'Answer—I had no idea about an Eighty-eighth Street apartment.'"

"'Question—You had no idea about an Eighty-eighth Street apartment?'"

"'Answer—That's right.'"

"'Question—Didn't you know that was where the girls were killed?'"

"'Answer—I didn't even know the address or place. I knew they were killed in Manhattan.'"

Keenan looked up from the transcript and fixed his eyes on DiPrima. "But you did know where the girls were killed when you were questioning George Whitmore, didn't you?" he demanded.

DiPrima let out a heavy sigh. "I knew they were killed in Manhattan." He blinked hard and then finished by saying, "And I knew they were killed on Eighty-eighth Street. Yes, sir."

Keenan bore in on the witness as he moved slowly toward him. Now just a few feet separating him from the witness, he shot out, "And you knew *that* when you were questioning George Whitmore?"

"Yes."

"And yet, you testified under oath, 'I didn't even know the address or the place.' You did testify that way?"

"Yes, sir."

The jury was riveted by the confrontation; and after DiPrima's admission, the jurors focused on Keenan. Exposed as a cop who had lied under oath, DiPrima's face blushed red. He kept his eyes on the prosecutor, as if he couldn't face the jurors any longer.

Keenan glared at the witness. *Checkmate,* Glass thought.

"Now, Detective DiPrima, was that the truth when you testified in Brooklyn?" Keenan asked.

"I can't answer that question without elaborating on it," DiPrima whined.

"You can't answer whether that was the truth without elaborating?" Keenan scoffed. "Why on earth not?"

"Because my answer of 'yes' would be misconstrued," DiPrima explained weakly.

Because your answer is that you committed perjury, Glass thought.

CHAPTER 23

One by one, Mack Dollinger put the Brooklyn cops on the stand to defend the case against Whitmore. And one by one, Keenan either dismissed their testimony as inconsequential or forced them to paint themselves as lazy, incompetent or dishonest. Then, at last, the defense attorney called Detective Edward Bulger.

The heavyweight championship bout is about to begin, Glass thought.

When the detective entered the courtroom, Glass was surprised how much Bulger had aged since he'd last seen him. The paunch was more pronounced, as were the jowls, which hung from the once-square jaw. He looked like he'd aged ten years since the early spring. Then again, "the hero," who'd solved that generation's most notorious murders in the New York metro area, had suffered repeated blows to his reputation and pride.

The downward spiral had started with the arrest of Richard Robles and the media blitz that had painted George Whitmore Jr. as an innocent scapegoat and his accusers as dirty racist cops. Then in April '65, shortly after the Edmonds mistrial, the NAACP brought to the attention of the press the story of David Coleman, an unemployed twenty-two-year-old black man living in Brooklyn when he was convicted in 1959 of the murder and rape of an elderly white woman, Margaret O'Meara. Detective Bulger had been the lead detective in that case, too, when they interrogated Coleman. After pleading his innocence for thirty-six hours, the suspect had finally confessed to the murder and nearly a hundred burglaries. Although he'd quickly recanted and accused the police of intimidating him, he was convicted and sentenced to death based almost solely on his confession.

Then shortly after the Edmonds mistrial, the NAACP uncovered another case of a questionable confession involving Detective Bulger. A murder suspect, Charles Everett, was told by Bulger that if he would admit to attacking the victim, who the detective claimed was still alive, Bulger would convince the victim to agree to a light sentence. Frightened, Everett decided to confess to assault and hope for the best. But the victim was dead, and Everett was charged with murder and convicted.

In light of the Whitmore allegations of Bulger's questionable conduct, both cases were currently being reviewed at the appellate court level, and the early consensus was that the convictions would be overturned. The disturbing similarity of the other two cases and Whitmore's was one of the main reasons cited when the legislature and Governor Rockefeller did away with the death penalty in July '65.

As Detective Bulger clenched his jaw and walked past the prosecution table, with his eyes fixed straight ahead, Mel Glass thought about the hours he and John Keenan had spent discussing the Brooklyn cops' motives. In the beginning they didn't believe that the Brooklyn detectives, Bulger in particular, had set about trying to frame an innocent man. Edward Bulger had seen the photograph and he'd been convinced that the blonde was Janice Wylie and that George Whitmore Jr. was her killer.

Whether it was from a real desire to see justice done, or to make himself a hero, or a little of both was up for discussion. After that sighting of the photograph, Bulger had done everything in his power to badger, cajole and trick an easily manipulated and compliant young man with a low IQ, an eighth-grade education and a pronounced naïveté into confessing.

And if that meant helping to refresh the suspect's memory by providing some of the details, then, well, the ends justified the means, didn't they? Glass thought ruefully.

After the revelations about the Coleman and Everett cases, the prosecutors wondered if they'd been giving Bulger too much of the benefit of the doubt about his motives. At the very least, the detective and his cohorts, who'd gone along for the ride, had been myopic and lazy. Captain Frank Weldon and Edward Bulger had both been told by Detective John Lynch in the early-morning hours of Saturday, April 25, 1964, that Max Wylie denied that the blonde in the photo was his daughter. It wouldn't have necessarily killed their case. The photograph could still have come from the apartment. However, the Brooklyn detectives and their bosses didn't take the next step and drive to Wildwood to see if Whitmore's story about the dump, or his alibi about being in the Ivy Hotel, held up. Neither had they tried to find the women in the photograph.

The detectives not only supplied Whitmore with the factual details of the murders through their leading questions, but they also directed him to the conclusions that determined his guilt. For example, when Whitmore told ADA James Hosty during the Q&A that the apartment building was four to five stories high, Bulger left the room. When the detective came back, he whispered in the prosecutor's ear.

Playing into the detective's determination to make Whitmore's statement fit the facts, Hosty then asked, "You mentioned that this building was about four to five stories high. Could it have been eight to ten stories?"

"Yes," Whitmore replied.

Then there was the anecdote about the razor blade wrapper that Bulger said he'd seen lying on the bathroom floor. The detective knew that a razor blade had been found on the floor of the murder room; at his suggestion Whitmore said he'd taken the blade out of a paper wrapper and used it to cut a sheet into strips to bind the girls—all details that had been supplied by Bulger and DiPrima. But the detective apparently didn't know that the razor blade had been from a dispenser found in a bedroom drawer; it never had a paper wrapper. So the ever-pleasing Whitmore had confessed to something that never happened—a story that could have only come from the detective.

Glass's and Keenan's concerns about the Brooklyn detectives' manipulation of Whitmore were further illuminated by two other anecdotes. In the first, during the afternoon questioning, Bulger had told Whitmore that he'd just spoken to the girls on the phone. Later, when Hosty took the Q&A in the early-morning hours of April 25, he asked Whitmore about the window shades being down.

"Why did you pull the shades down?" Hosty had asked.

"If they came to, they would get up," Whitmore had replied.

"The two girls you cut?"

"Yes, and somebody in the next apartment would see them tied up."

"You were afraid somebody from the outside could look into the apartment?"

"Yes."

When Glass and Keenan read about this exchange, they were astounded. Anyone who had attacked and brutally murdered the girls—especially in the manner in which it was done—would have known that scenario was inconceivable.

Significantly, the Hosty Q&A started at two in the morning and ended fifty minutes later on April 25. Not satisfied with the faux confession, the interrogators had reconvened the session at

4:03 *A.M.* Whitmore had claimed to have cut Janice Wylie "a few times around the face." Given the medical examiner's description that Janice Wylie was disemboweled and Emily Hoffert virtually decapitated, the detectives and Hosty needed a more evidentiary consistent confession:

"Now you originally told me that you cut her (Janice Wylie) a few times around the face?" Hosty then asked.

"Yes."

"And was that correct?"

"No."

"Where did you cut her?"

"In the stomach."

"How did you cut her around the stomach?"

"Sliced."

"How many times did you slice her?"

"Two or three times."

Keenan and Glass were stunned and appalled at the manipulation. They believed that between the end of the initial Q&A and its resumption more than an hour later, Whitmore had been given answers that once again fit the evidence. So after having a suspect in custody for eighteen hours, during which time George Whitmore Jr. was continually questioned, Detective Edward Bulger got what he felt he needed to be the sleuth who solved the notorious "Career Girls Murders."

Detective Bulger's appearance in the courtroom was not by his choice. In fact, he'd tried to avoid showing up despite having been subpoenaed. In the days before his scheduled appearance, he'd "disappeared" and couldn't be located when Detective Lynch was sent to find him.

The defense and NYPD had even asked Bulger's son, who was also a detective, but he said he didn't know where his father had gone. Believing that the son was less than sincere, Glass insisted that he be brought before Judge Davidson in his chambers and ordered to contact his father. Davidson was not the sort of judge who put up with any shenanigans. He glared at the son, who then declared that "by coincidence" he'd heard from his father the night before. "He's waiting for my call at a motel in Miami," the son said.

"Then I suggest you call him and tell him to be in court tomorrow at ten A.M. sharp. Am I clear?" Judge Davidson demanded.

"Yes, sir, very clear," the son responded.

The order worked. Bulger now sat in the witness chair and explained to the jury that he'd recently retired from the force, but he had been a detective first grade with the Brooklyn North Homicide Squad on April 24, 1964, and into the morning of April 25, when he questioned George Whitmore about the Wylie-Hoffert slayings.

Like Joseph DiPrima before him, Edward Bulger recounted the events that eventually led to Whitmore's arrest for the murders. And, he said, no one threatened George Whitmore Jr. or told him what to say. "I made out a statement for George Whitmore to sign. He initialed each page and signed the last one."

On cross-examination Keenan made sure that the jury understood that Detective Bulger had been assigned to the Wylie-Hoffert task force for about three months, much longer than most other detectives similarly situated, except for the detectives originally assigned to the case. As such, he'd made himself an expert, or so he might have thought, on every aspect of the murders: he read all of the DD5s, viewed all of the crime scene photographs numerous times and had spent multiple hours on various occasions inside apartment 3C at 57 East Eighty-Eighth Street.

Keenan also got Bulger to note that Whitmore did not have a lawyer present at the Seventy-third Precinct when he confessed. He knew the jury would remember that Richard Robles did have a lawyer available when he decided to make statements to David Downes and the other Manhattan detectives.

Now, as in the second Joe Louis–Max Schmeling heavyweight fight in Yankee Stadium, the initial fundamental sparring was to be mere prelude as Keenan moved abruptly to the knockout. He asked the detective to describe his interviewing style. "You are always polite, soft-spoken, calm, and you don't feed the suspect any information?"

"Yes, sir."

Walking over to the jury box ledge to examine his notes, Keenan appeared to be reading when he asked: "Do you recall questioning Eddie White, a black man, about twenty-four years of age, about the Wylie-Hoffert murders on December 16, 1963?"

"I remember vaguely talking to him," Bulger replied, frowning.

"Do you recall saying to Mr. White as you leaned across the desk in the presence of Sergeant Brent, of the Twenty-third Detective Squad, and hitting your hand on the desk"—as he spoke, Keenan's voice grew louder and angrier; everyone in the courtroom seemed to jump when he slammed his hand on the ledge, where he kept his notes—"and saying to Mr. White, 'You're the guy who did this! You saw the door open and walked in. You saw the bottles on the floor and picked them up! Then you saw Janice . . . nude!'"

Bulger's jaw set as he glared at Keenan. "No, sir!"

"Do you recall Sergeant Brent looking at you after you said that to Mr. White?"

"No, sir."

"Do you recall saying to Mr. White then, 'All right, get out of here, but I'm not through with you yet'? Do you recall saying any such thing?"

"No, sir."

"You deny that happened?"

"No, sir."

"You don't deny that happened?"

"I do deny it happened."

As the witness stewed, Keenan lowered his voice. He moved on to People's Exhibit 72, the photograph of Abbe Mills and Jennifer Holley.

Bulger acknowledged that Whitmore first told him he got the photograph at the Wildwood dump, and that he'd written the inscription on the back.

"And you responded how?" Keenan asked.

"I told him I didn't believe him."

"Were you watching George Whitmore's stomach?"

The question caught everyone except Glass off guard. Bulger furrowed his brow. "I don't know."

"But you didn't believe him," Keenan suggested, shrugging.

"Yes, sir."

"You thought he was lying."

"Yes, sir."

Now direct and assertive, Keenan asked, "Well, didn't you tell my colleague Mel Glass on July 30, 1964, in room 617 of the District Attorney's Office in New York County that you could always tell when a Negro was lying by watching his stomach because it moves in and out when he lies?"

It seemed that for a moment everyone in the courtroom held his or her breath. There were quite a few black spectators in the courtroom, and their faces contorted into scowls. Angry muttering rose to such a level that Judge Davidson had to put a stop to it with a stern look.

"I don't remember," Bulger replied.

"You don't remember?"

"I'm not saying I didn't say it, but I don't remember saying it. I may have said it."

As Keenan's questioning went on, Bulger seemed to wear down. He claimed it was Joseph DiPrima who demanded that George Whitmore Jr. tell the truth and quit saying he got the photograph from the dump. "Then Whitmore said he got it in the apartment on Eighty-eighth Street in Manhattan."

Bulger, however, insisted that Whitmore mentioned the Eighty-eighth Street apartment before anyone else discussed the address.

The detective denied that Whitmore was badgered for hours before he began to make admissions. "It was maybe a half hour," he said.

But Keenan pointed out that Bulger told James Hosty it had been an hour.

"I was all mixed-up," Bulger claimed.

"But you didn't say you were mixed-up when you saw Mr. Glass in July 1964 and said there were no errors in the summary you wrote for Hosty," Keenan noted.

"That's because I needed to refresh my memory," Bulger retorted. "I got straightened out talking to the other detectives."

"And that was more accurate than the summary you wrote for Mr. Hosty three days after Whitmore's arrest?" Keenan asked.

During question after question, Keenan demonstrated the efforts Bulger made to make Whitmore's admissions fit the facts—such as when Whitmore was asked by the detective what time he left Brooklyn to travel to the Upper East Side.

"He said ten A.M., which you knew would not have given him enough time," Keenan pointed out. "You asked him if it wasn't more like eight-thirty, because you knew the clock radio had stopped at ten thirty-seven."

"Around that time, yes, sir. Approximately that time, yes, sir."

Nearing the end of his cross-examination, Keenan moved on to whether Bulger had told Whitmore that the victims were still alive.

"Now, Mr. Bulger, did you or anybody in your presence, any detective or any official, tell Whitmore that the girls were alive?" Keenan asked.

"No, sir. Not to my knowledge, not in my presence."

"Nobody told Whitmore that the girls were alive?"

"Not that I know of."

Keenan continued to pursue the point. "So you don't recall whether Whitmore was told the girls were alive?"

"I don't recall it," Bulger replied, with his eyes flicking back and forth among all the jurors and Keenan.

"Whitmore told you the reason he pulled down the shade after he had cut the girls, and after he tied them up, was because he was afraid they would get up?"

"That's what he said."

"Didn't that indicate to you, Mr. Bulger, that Whitmore thought the girls were alive?"

"That's what he said."

Keenan relentlessly pressed again. "Did you ever tell Whitmore that you had just talked to the two girls on the telephone and that they weren't mad at him, that they had only been in the hospital a short time?"

"I'm not sure. I might have."

"You might have said that to Whitmore?"

"I might have," Bulger replied defensively. "I might have."

"You might have told Whitmore that you might have just talked to the two girls, Janice Wylie and Emily Hoffert. You might have said that to him?"

"I can't remember."

"What is your best recollection? Did you?"

"I say I might have."

"You might have?"

"Yes."

"And if you did, that was a lie, wasn't it?"

"Well, it's all the way you look at it."

As Keenan wrapped up, Edward Bulger sat in the witness chair with his head down. *Defeated*, Glass thought, but he felt no pity for the detective or his colleague Joseph DiPrima.

It wasn't just how they'd conducted their investigation, Glass thought. But what really rankled him was that they'd also been unwilling to concede when faced with the facts that they'd made a mistake.

In fact, they were so concerned about their egos and reputations, Mel Glass believed, that they were willing to provide the real killer with his defense. Or as he'd said to John Keenan before he began to cross-examine Bulger, "They'd rather see a vicious predator like Robles set free on the streets, and send an innocent man to prison for life, than admit they were wrong."

CHAPTER 24

Sitting at the prosecution table, Mel Glass seethed. He tried not to show it, but his eyes hardened as he followed Mack Dollinger's movements in front of the jury as the defense attorney delivered his final summation.

What had set Glass off was that the tall, handsome and capable man exhorting the jury to acquit his client had once worked for Frank Hogan. Dollinger knew the ethics that Hogan demanded of his attorneys. Yet, he had just accused the New York DAO of framing Richard Robles, which was as vile as it was absurd. The most galling aspect was that Dollinger knew better. In fact, Dollinger had reason to know since the night of Robles's arrest on January 26, 1965, that his client was as guilty as sin.

When Glass left Robles in the holding area that evening to speak to Mack Dollinger, Glass told the defense attorney everything the young killer had just admitted: "'It wasn't panic. Something went wrong.'"

Dollinger had then spoken to Robles and, leaving his client with David Downes, approached Glass with an offer: "My client just confirmed everything you told me. We're willing to accept a plea to murder, but no death penalty."

Mel Glass shook his head. "I can't make that commitment."

"Then let me talk to Al Herman," Dollinger suggested.

"Talk to anybody you want, including Hogan," Glass responded.

The defense attorney had then gone back to Robles, who, in his attorney's absence, had confessed to Downes and the other cops who'd entered the room. There was no claim or anything to suggest that anyone had threatened his client, or abused him, or tricked him into anything. Simply put, Robles's guilty conscience had gotten the best of him finally.

Glass had no objection to a defense lawyer zealously representing his client and forcing the prosecution to prove guilt beyond a reasonable doubt. It was the crucible, the sine qua non, of the truth-finding trial process. That was as it should be. But to know that his client had committed the murders, and yet turn around and obfuscate the truth to the jury about the alleged venal motives of the police and DAO—actually stoop so low as to accuse them, with no factual basis in the record, of committing crimes to frame his client—well, that went beyond the pale, Glass believed.

It was clear to Glass that Dollinger was desperate. In both his examination and cross-examination of the witnesses, John Keenan had carefully debunked George Whitmore Jr.'s confession, while demonstrating why Richard Robles's incriminating admissions were to be believed.

Reaching deep into his arsenal of advocacy, Dollinger conjured up what many defense attorneys resort to when the facts and the law do not support their cause: the frame defense.

"The district attorney's office felt that the case against George Whitmore wasn't strong enough because that piece of circumstantial evidence—that photograph that George Whitmore said came from the apartment—they found out couldn't have come from the apartment," Dollinger said. "They felt that the inconsistency in the George Whitmore story made the case against Whitmore something they would prefer not to try."

Dollinger walked over to stand in front of the prosecution table. "The Delaneys were their deliverance, because only through the Delaneys could they possibly get somebody else to stand in for George Whitmore," he said. "And perhaps save the honor of the police department. They had to get a stand-in and they didn't care if it made sense or not."

Shaking his head as he glanced at Keenan and Glass, Dollinger continued. "If Robles were not an addict, if he were a human being like you or me or somebody else, do you think he would be on trial in this case? Do you think he would be the person that they would ask you to convict? Do you think that they would suggest to you that based on this evidence, on these facts, that this man is guilty if he was not an addict? He's a perfect patsy for the police, perfect."

Mack Dollinger whirled and walked back to stand next to his client. "Who is going to come to his defense? Who is going to scream and yell about him? Who cares about an addict? Who cares?"

Patting Robles on the shoulder, he added, "When they find, or if they find, the right man, then the prosecution will offer Mr. Gynt as their witness and not leave it for the defense to offer him as ours."

Mel Glass was still seething when court recessed for the afternoon and he went back to the office with John Keenan to prepare for the People's summation the next day. The skull session began with Glass shaking his head and blasting Mack Dollinger's tactics in frustration and anger.

"John, maybe I'm in the wrong business," he lamented to his colleague. "I've been at this for seven years, tried scores of felons for all kinds of mayhem they perpetrate on innocent people, and have heard all sorts of excuses from defense attorneys. But listening to Dollinger's summation was such an incredible outrage—a position that is so contrary to the truth."

As Glass paced about the office, Keenan took a seat and let his younger colleague vent. "Two girls get slaughtered and the defendant's admissions are completely corroborated," Glass went on. "And with no evidence, just rank speculation, Dollinger tells the court and jury that we framed his client. And how do we do it? According to the defense, we picked out two people, the Delaneys, who we don't know, who have criminal records up the wazoo, and we tell them to tell us to incriminate someone we don't know. And, of course, we are so venal, we let the real killer roam the streets with impunity. And this 'patsy,' this so-called stand-in, Robles, who we don't know from borscht, lo and behold, makes admissions on tape that corroborates what he told Downes, the police brass and the Delaneys. What a coincidence! And this nonsense with Gynt, the doorman? Give me a break here!"

Glass sat down on a club chair. "And let's get this straight, the only reason Gynt appears in this case is because we presented him to the defense on a silver platter. The defense knows that the reason we didn't call him is because of the conflicting versions he gave about what, if anything, he saw and heard. And he's totally unreliable."

Sighing, Glass looked at Keenan. "And, John, what really rankles me are the Brooklyn cops. Instead of admitting they made a mistake, they circled the wagons, stuck to their stories that Whitmore is the guy and gave Robles a complete defense."

Glass threw his hands up in the air. "What in the hell is happening to our justice system!"

It appeared that Glass had run out of steam, so Keenan chose that moment to speak. "It's okay, Mel. We made a mistake and we're paying for it. But what you did was restore the credibility of our office and everything the justice system is about. We're going to convict this fine fellow, and we have you to thank for it."

Glass looked over at Keenan, one of the best of the best, who'd won scores of murder convictions in his career. Keenan was smiling, and suddenly Glass felt humbled. He grinned.

"Okay, okay . . . let's talk summation," Keenan suggested.

"I think you start with showing again why Whitmore's confession is untrustworthy," Glass said as he began to tick off the reasons. "John, it's not just that what Whitmore said was inconsistent with certain facts, the scenario he was presenting doesn't square with what happened. He's connecting dots that have been laid out by the Brooklyn cops. For example, Bulger tells him that he just spoke to the girls and they're alive. So what does Whitmore do? He says he pulled down the window shade because he was afraid they might get up after he stabbed them. But the real killer knows damn well that these girls, after he butchered them, would never be standing up again, much less be alive."

Keenan tapped the legal pad he'd been making notes on. "And, of course, Mel, the killer would have known right then that the cops were lying. But not George Whitmore, because he had no reason to believe otherwise."

Glass nodded. "Then Bulger's got Whitmore going through the lobby door that doesn't open, with no Exit sign on it, leading to God knows where, and gets knives from a kitchen table that doesn't exist. Oh . . . and he said he entered the apartment through a service door that Kate Olsen testified was bolted locked."

Glass paused and rubbed his chin. "And let's not forget the Whitmore Q&A with Hosty. It first starts at two A.M. and ends at two-fifty in the morning. Then an hour goes by and they pick it up again at four oh-three and this one ends at four-twelve A.M. And here's another example of the Brooklyn cops trying to conform Whitmore to some immutable facts—like what Robles really did to the two girls."

Picking up a copy of the Q&A that recommenced at 4:03 *A.M.*, Glass read:

Question: Now, George, I'd like to clear one further thing up. You originally told me you cut her a few times around the face?

Answer: Yes.

Question: Was that correct?

Answer: No.

Question: Where do you cut her?

Answer: In the stomach.

Question: How did you cut her around the stomach?

Answer: Sliced.

Question: How many times did you slice her on the stomach?

Answer: Two or three times.

Glass flipped the Q&A onto the conference table. "Bulger knew from seeing those crime scene photos of the deceased that Janice Wylie was disemboweled. So, of course, he wasn't satisfied with Whitmore saying he cut her around the face. I wonder what happened in the hour or so in between the two sessions. It's a classic example of someone talking about a case that's totally separate from reality."

Then there's the photograph, Glass noted, which was the sole reason Detective Edward Bulger thought to question Whitmore about Wylie-Hoffert. "If he'd stopped and thought it through, Bulger would have known it didn't make any sense. What killer is going to keep something of significant evidentiary value, a photograph, allegedly of the deceased no less, tying him to the murders, for eight months and write, 'To George From Louise' on the back so that he could show it to his friends? Keep a photograph of the victim in the most infamous murder in the city, show it around, bragging, 'This is my girlfriend,' and not worrying that someone might say, 'Hey, that's Janice Wylie'?

"It was a disgrace," Glass pointed out, "for Bulger to ignore Lynch's report from Max Wylie that the blonde in the photograph wasn't his daughter."

Glass noted the substantial difference between Whitmore's reaction to the accusations and that of Robles. Throughout his interrogation Whitmore either quietly denied his complicity, asked to go home or repeated what the detectives had fed to him in a dry monotone.

"Compare that to Robles who broke down crying," Glass said. "And says after he confesses, 'I don't want to talk about it anymore. Please, I want to erase it from my mind.' Which one sounds like he has a guilty conscience?"

Just as he'd once set up the mosaic of the prosecution case, the next day, Keenan methodically placed each tile together leading to the full picture revealing the guilt of the defendant "beyond any and all doubt." As Glass sat in his seat and ticked off the points on his legal pad, Keenan took command of the space in front of the jury, laying out each.

"Isn't it perfectly clear that Whitmore had about as much to do with killing Janice Wylie and Emily Hoffert as Abbe Mills did?" Keenan asked the jury. "Mr. Whitmore was Trilby and Bulger was Svengali, and that's the way it worked. . . . I submit to you that Mr. Whitmore doesn't have the vaguest idea what happened to him that night in the Seventy-third [Precinct] Detective Squad."

Keenan followed through on his conversation with Mel Glass that the Whitmore statements were totally disconnected from reality—that they weren't merely inconsistencies.

"So let's look at Whitmore's route home to Brooklyn," John Keenan said. "That is the most magical part of the whole Whitmore statement, it's from *Alice in Wonderland*. From Eighty-eighth Street he walks back to Forty-second Street. He takes the subway home from Forty-second Street to Brooklyn. He gets out of the subway, walks to his house about eight and a half blocks from the subway station. And what does he do? He sits on his stoop. And then what does he do? He goes to his uncle's house to borrow money to buy a hot dog."

Keenan held his arms akimbo and, shaking his head, exclaimed, "Where's the blood? Where was the blood on Whitmore? It wasn't on Whitmore. It was on Robles's left trouser leg. It was on the green shirt that was in the paper bag when he got to the Delaneys' and had saturated through to the T-shirt underneath. That's why there was no blood on Whitmore."

Keenan picked up the Q&A statement and held it up for the jury to see. "The blood wasn't on Whitmore, who in this statement said that he took the knives from the kitchen table drawer. The blood wasn't on that man. You know why? Maybe you forgot this. There wasn't a kitchen table in the kitchen, so there couldn't have been a drawer. . . . Remember when I asked Bulger about the lobby door that led to the service stairway? He told you he didn't know very much about that door. Kate Olsen testified she didn't even know where that door led to. But Whitmore went through the locked door with the nonexistent Exit sign, leading in his mind to God knows where, and gets knives once allegedly inside the apartment from a kitchen table that doesn't exist."

Keenan turned and pointed at the defendant. "And when you blow the Whitmore smoke away, do you know who sits in front of you? Richard Robles."

Turning back to the jury, Keenan changed direction. "Now let's start talking about some of the affirmative evidence here and let's put the smoke behind us. Let's talk about the Delaneys. What can you say about the Delaneys? They're no angels. They're not pillars of the community. They're not, in Mr. Dollinger's words, bank vice presidents. The Delaneys told you, a friend of theirs—not an enemy, a friend of theirs—not someone they had a grudge against, but a friend, the common-law husband of Mrs. Delaney's aunt. They tell you that Robles, their friend, admitted the killings to them."

Keenan put his hands on his hips as he looked at the jurors and rocked back a little on his heels. "I told you in the very beginning of my summation, of my introductory remarks, that a trial is a search for the truth under the rules of evidence. So how do we know that the Delaneys are telling us the truth? Do you think that the Delaneys knew that Abbe Mills, the girl in People's seventy-two in evidence, had been located? Do you think the Delaneys knew that? As a matter of fact, for all the Delaneys knew, and for all anybody in the public knew, for all the world knew, other than certain police officers and certain district attorneys, and quite obviously Abbe Mills, for all anybody knew, the case was solved and it was George Whitmore. Why should the Delaneys mention a solved case? Why should they mention a case that was closed? Why? Because they really knew something about it, that's why."

Glancing at the defense table, Keenan went on with his summation. "Now the defense suggests in this Machiavellian frame scenario that Robles was made a stand-in for Whitmore. And that somehow the Delaneys got into this act and suddenly the Delaneys came up with Robles's name. How did this all happen? Did the detectives go up to Jimmy Delaney and say, 'Hey, Delaney, listen. We've got to build a case against somebody because the police department is embarrassed because of this Whitmore situation.' Did somebody go up to Delaney and say, 'We want you to give us some information on a case you don't know anything about. Hey, but don't worry, we'll give you the information and then you give it back to us. And then you come to an assistant district attorney and you tell it to him.' Is that the way it happened? Where is there any evidence of this?"

Keenan furrowed his brow and shook his head. "Why does Delaney give Robles's name, unless Robles is the killer? Why does he pick on a friend? And if it's a frame, why in the world does Delaney involve his wife? If this is a frame-up, a concocted story between the Delaneys as to the defendant coming to their house, why would Jimmy Delaney complicate it by getting his wife involved? He certainly wouldn't involve his own wife because he knew his own wife was the niece of Robles's common-law wife. He wouldn't have involved Mrs. Delaney. You know why he said his wife was there? Because she was there. Do you know why Delaney said he went to buy narcotics? Because he did go buy narcotics and left his wife there. But the truth makes sense. Where would Robles go after killing these two girls? Would he go to the home of a bank vice president? Or would he go to the home of friends who can give him what he needs right then—first a fix and then a change of clothes."

Looking each juror in the face, Keenan then moved forward up to the jury rail. "Lest there be any doubt about the credibility of the Delaneys, we know from the testimony and how this case unfolded that the Delaneys are telling us the truth, the whole truth. We know this, don't we? And from the evidence you know how and why. In their statement that the Delaneys made on October 19, 1964, they told Mel Glass that when recounting what Robles said to them, they recalled that he said that during the course of the murders the odor was awful. We know from the testimony of chief medical examiner Dr. Helpern that because Robles punctured Janice Wylie's intestines three times, there was emitted into the room a foul odor. So the science of this case, as testified to by Dr. Helpern, a world-renowned forensic pathologist, corroborates, beyond any and all doubt, what the Delaneys told us that the defendant told them. So either they're absolutely telling us the truth, or they had a crystal ball and made it up out of thin air and forecasted the future—they forecasted the scientific analysis. We also know from the evidence that there were absolutely no police reports that made notice of any odor in that room. So much for the defense suggestion that the Delaneys are merely puppets in this fantasy conspiracy to frame the defendant."

Keenan walked over to the prosecution table and picked up the photograph of a rear view of the building at 57 East Eighty-eighth Street showing the protruding vents and kitchen windows. He held it up for the jury. "How do we know that Detective Downes, Lieutenant Sullivan and Sergeant Brent testified truthfully about the defendant's confessions to them in the clerical office located on the second floor of the Twenty-third [Precinct] Detective Squad room on the night of January twenty-sixth of this year? They testified that Robles told them that he entered the apartment by climbing through the kitchen window. The testimony in the record is that right after Robles confessed, the police went to 57 East Eighty-eighth Street and checked out the exterior area, looking at the vents in relationship to the kitchen windows. And two days later, photos were taken. So what did they do that night when Robles told them, 'I went through the window'? They went over to the building. If he didn't make those admissions, why would they have gone over to the building to look? Why would they take the photos? Is this part of what the defense wants you to believe that there's a master conspiratorial plan? There is no evidence of it. Logic and common sense suggests, supported by the evidence, that the police are telling the truth."

Keenan wrapped up by talking about the tapes. "Now remember when you heard the tapes that contained the recorded conversations between the Delaneys and the defendant in their apartment, and on one of them you heard Robles say to the Delaneys, 'If I could only plant in my mind that you made this up, and it really didn't happen, like I would take that test.' And he was referring to the lie detector test. Do you remember Robles then said, 'I can't beat a lie detector test.' He couldn't plant it in his mind, because it did happen, and because they, the Delaneys, did not make it up. He did kill the two girls. That's why he broke down and cried when questioned by the detectives. And that's why he said he was relieved when he learned that Whitmore had been arrested."

Walking over to the defense table and standing directly in front of Richard Robles, John Keenan continued his speech. "Ladies and gentlemen, in his own words, the defendant, Robles, incontrovertibly stamps himself and marks himself the killer, not beyond a reasonable doubt, but beyond any and all doubt. Never forget that tape, in evidence, when Robles says to the Delaneys, 'If only I could plant in my mind that this didn't happen.' But he can't plant it there, and it can't be planted in your minds, because it did happen and because he did it."

Glaring at Robles, Keenan's voice rose. "This is not just some homicide case, not some stabbing, shooting or ligature strangulation, although all serious and horrible. We all now know that this murder case was a deplorable outrage, a slaughter, an annihilation, and"—now John Keenan pointed his finger at the defendant, whose face drained of all color—"the annihilator sits right here, the defendant, Robles."

EPILOGUE

It took the jury of eight men and four women just six hours to reach a verdict. The spectator gallery, which had been packed throughout the trial, had less than a dozen people in the seats—most of them reporters—when the foreman declared, "We find the defendant guilty as charged."

It was December 1, 1965. A month later, Richard Robles was back in court for sentencing on two counts of murder. Asked if he had anything to say before the court pronounced its decision, he cried out, "All I can say, Your Honor, is that I did not kill those girls. I'm going to jail for something I did not do!" Unmoved, Judge Davidson sentenced him to the maximum the law permitted: life in prison.

For the next twenty-one years, Robles insisted he was innocent and had been framed by the New York DAO and NYPD. Indeed, many people continued to believe that George Whitmore Jr. had committed the crimes, both in Brooklyn and in Manhattan, or that perhaps he and Robles had committed them together.

Then in 1986, at a hearing before a parole board, Robles announced that he had undergone a spiritual rebirth. And now he wanted to set the record straight.

As he'd told the Delaneys and Detective David Downes, Robles explained to the commissioners that he only planned to commit a burglary when he climbed in through the third-floor kitchen window on 57 East Eighty-eighth Street.

"Miss Wylie was in the apartment. I tied her up. She was nude, and I wanted to have sex with her," Robles revealed.

Later, when Emily Hoffert told him that she was going to remember his face and that he was going to jail, Robles said he decided he couldn't leave witnesses, who might identify him. "The thought entered my mind. I had to kill. I was out of it."

When it was over, Robles said, he staggered into the bathroom and looked in the mirror. "The blood had drained from my face. I was like a ghost. . . . I was a ghost. . . . I don't know how to describe what I was feeling."

As of the writing of this book, Richard Robles remains incarcerated in the New York State prison system.

As for George Whitmore Jr., the nightmare continued for years. After testifying at the Richard Robles trial, he was sent back to jail to await his own retrials in Brooklyn for the Edmonds and Estrada cases.

However, before either got under way again, the U.S. Supreme Court, having heard arguments in a case known as *Miranda* v. *State of Arizona*, handed down on June 13, 1966, a monumental Fifth Amendment due process, fundamental-fairness decision safeguarding a suspect's rights against self-incrimination. The court ruled that suspects subjected to "custodial interrogation" would have to be informed by their law enforcement interrogators that they had the right to remain silent, that anything they said could be used against them in court, that they had the right to have an attorney present during any questioning. If they could not afford an attorney, one would be provided to them. It did not prevent police from questioning suspects or using the information they gained to further their investigation; however, failure to provide the warnings meant the information could not be used in court against the defendant.

In reaching their decision, the Supreme Court justices cited the experiences of George Whitmore Jr. Writing for the majority opinion, Chief Justice Earl Warren stated that courts must be on guard against false confessions gained by police through intimidation or coercion when the suspect was not afforded counsel: *The most recent conspicuous example occurred in New York, in 1964, when a Negro of limited intelligence confessed to two brutal murders and a rape which he had not committed.*

The court's decision would have a profound and far-reaching effect on the way in which police conducted interrogations from that point on. It also had a personal impact on the life of George Whitmore Jr.

In Brooklyn, a new district attorney announced that in light of concerns regarding the questioning of Whitmore by Brooklyn detectives, as well as legal opinions that the Miranda warnings could be applied retroactively, his office would no longer pursue trying him for the murder of Minnie Edmonds.

However, it was not so simple in the Estrada case. Even if the defendant's statements to the detectives could not be used, they still had an eyewitness, the victim, who maintained that Whitmore was the man who attacked her. And Whitmore had been convicted of the crime, even if it had been overturned. The district attorney decided that the only fair thing to do for the victim was to retry the case and let a jury decide.

In July, George Whitmore Jr. was again tried for the attempted rape/assault of Alma Estrada. She once again took the stand and implicated Whitmore, who this time did not take the stand in his defense. Based on Estrada's testimony and that of police officer

Tommy Micelli, whose "spontaneous" conversation with a young man in a Laundromat did not fall under the Miranda warnings, Whitmore was again convicted.

Whitmore was sentenced to five to ten years in prison. This time he was sent to Sing Sing penitentiary.

However, his attorneys did not give up. After seven months they were able to get him out of prison while his case was appealed on several technicalities. But the appeal could only look at a very narrow set of issues that had occurred during the trial, and not the entire case. In 1971, the New York Court of Appeals ruled four to three to uphold the conviction, though the dissenting judges were harsh in their condemnation of the Brooklyn police and the Kings County District Attorney's Office, suggesting that their conduct was one of "misconduct and ineptitude."

Whitmore's bond was revoked and he was sent back to prison in February 1972. It wasn't long, however, before new allegations of official misconduct in the Alma Estrada case were raised. Defense investigators uncovered the fact that the Brooklyn District Attorney's Office withheld crucial evidence from the defense, including: Estrada had made contradictory statements to police officers regarding her identification of Whitmore; a relative claimed Estrada had originally identified another man; most damning, the FBI analysis of the button and thread Estrada tore from her assailant's coat did not match the buttons and thread from Whitmore's coat, as the prosecution had intimated at trial.

District Attorney Frank Hogan, ADA John Keenan and ADA Mel Glass made several attempts to persuade the Brooklyn DA to exonerate George Whitmore Jr. He was finally released from prison on April 10, 1973. Not counting the time he was out on bond, he spent almost three and a half years in jails and prisons for crimes he did not commit.

The legendary district attorney Frank Hogan remained in office for thirty-two years. He suffered a stroke in August 1973 and died in February 1974, leaving behind an office known for its integrity, professionalism and the even-handed application of the law to all.

John Keenan became head of the Felony Trial Bureau and then later the chief of the Homicide Bureau. In 1983, he was appointed as United States Federal District Court judge for the Southern District of New York. Like his dear friend and colleague, Mel Glass, Keenan has served on the bench, as he similarly performed in the Frank Hogan DAO, with grace, dignity and courage.

Although their reputations were damaged by the Whitmore investigation, and there were calls for criminal charges of malfeasance and perjury, the Brooklyn detectives were never held accountable. They continued to maintain that they did nothing wrong. No one, however, was ever able to explain how exactly George Whitmore Jr. was able to give a detailed confession and then a sixty-one-page Q&A statement to ADA James Hosty to a crime he didn't commit, or draw a diagram of an apartment he'd never been in.

Along with the Miranda warnings, the Whitmore snafu would continue to reverberate down through the years. It marked the beginning of a ten-year ordeal of racial tension, riots and turmoil in the city. The reputation of the NYPD suffered a tremendous blow, particularly in the black community, from which it never completely recovered.

Mel Glass became the youngest bureau chief ever appointed by Frank Hogan, first as the chief of the Complaint Bureau, and then the chief of the Criminal Courts Bureau, where he was also responsible for the training of new ADAs. In 1973, he was appointed a criminal court judge and thereafter an acting New York Supreme Court justice, where his service spanned two decades. While on the bench, he distinguished himself as a brilliant jurist not only for his encyclopedic knowledge of the law, but also for his even-handed fairness and respect for the maintenance and enhancement of the dignity of the justice system. His passion to do justice never waned. He passed away in May 2010, surrounded by his loving and devoted children and grandchildren.

For all of the damage Richard Robles did to other lives when "something went wrong" on August 28, 1963, none was greater than what he did to Max Wylie. In the years following the trials, Wylie's wife, Lambert, and his older daughter, Pamela, both died of cancer.

In 1975, alone, grieving and unable to remove the images of his daughter's brutalized body, and that of Emily Hoffert, from his mind, Max Wylie placed the barrel of a .38-caliber gun against the side of his head and pulled the trigger.

POSTSCRIPT

Classics are ageless. They don't wither in time. For them, there is no statute of limitations. They are intrinsically an expression and reflection of a value system and culture.

At their most compelling, they suggest a moral dimension that exists and ought to influence and determine the decisions that we make in our private and public lives. Certainly, public officials are mandated pursuant to our founding documents, the Declaration of Independence/Constitution—two promissory notes, if you will—to be guided by and act consonant with these moral and legal precepts. Unfortunately, all too frequently, the historical experience suggests otherwise.

Yet, there are heroes amongst us. Frank Hogan, Mel Glass and John Keenan qualify, in my judgment, as Arthurian knights of the Round Table. From them, I witnessed up close and personal the actual functioning of the inner sanctum of a ministry of justice operating on a case-by-case, qualitative analytical, apolitical merit-driven basis.

DA Frank Hogan was truly a legend long before Wylie-Hoffert occurred. Once convinced that Mel Glass's gut instincts and subsequent investigation were legit, and that George Whitmore Jr. was wrongfully indicted for the most gruesome and sensationalized double murders and rape in the media's radar, Hogan was prepared to admit his mistake, possibly fracture his career's reputation and exonerate an impoverished young man with an IQ lower than 70. And why? Simply and manifestly, because it was right; justice demanded it.

I first met Mel Glass and Frank Hogan during the interview hiring process. After my interview with Mel, I was sent to Hogan for final evaluation based upon his recommendation.

Having just graduated from law school at Berkeley, I returned home to New York, took the bar and started working at the Manhattan DA's Office. For the first three years of my tenure, I served in the Complaint and Criminal Courts Bureaus, mentored by my bureau chief, Mel Glass. He instilled in me the basics, the fundamentals of the blocking and tackling of precisely how to administer justice. He always held firm to the ideal that the two most important responsibilities of the DA are to exonerate the unjustly accused and proceed to prosecution only when there is unquestioned factual guilt corroborated by legally admissible evidence sufficient to convict the defendant beyond a reasonable doubt.

Mel Glass always avoided media exploitation. He never sought to capitalize monetarily or otherwise from, as he put it, "simply doing my job." After the conviction of Richard Robles in Wylie-Hoffert, Mel turned down an offer of $150,000 from *Life* magazine to reveal the "real" inside story.

After several years I graduated from Mel's tutelage, while serving in the Criminal Courts Bureau, to the elite corps, the Homicide Bureau. There I was mentored by John Keenan. How fortunate was I to be trained by Mel Glass and John Keenan? Sort of like playing at Notre Dame under Ara Parseghian and then to Green Bay coached by Vince Lombardi.

From Mel, it was all about the basics; from Keenan, it was the precision, drama and art of trial practice. He was truly a master, without equal.

To Frank Hogan, Mel Glass and John Keenan, I owe my professional career.

Approximately four years ago, Mel asked me to write this book. After all that had been written, he wanted the true story to be known. He supplied me with the actual trial transcripts, some of which is quoted in *Echoes of My Soul*, crime scene photos, police reports, autopsy protocols, his contemporaneous notes and other investigative material. Most valuable, however, were his insights and detailed recollections of the events. We spent countless months going over the material, which was voluminous. Throughout all the time we shared going over the case, his only admonition was that I must always remain *objective*. I have endeavored to do just that.

On one level *Echoes of My Soul* speaks volumes about how a committed individual, Mel Glass, can make a huge impact. A triumphant, uplifting justice victory delivered by a dedicated young Hogan acolyte, whose soul was pure, intact and righteous.

Yet *Echoes of My Soul* is much more meaningful. To do justice in our lives, to be civil, tolerant, rational and forthright is to enhance the dignity not only of ourselves but of the public office we may occupy, the job we hold and the culture in which we thrive. Those values are timeless. We need to experience them so that we may always be reminded who we are and from where we came. When faced with cultural coarsening, we seek affirmation of triumph. *Echoes of My Soul* satisfies that need.

Sometimes it is necessary to remind ourselves of the authenticity of American exceptionalism. We are a moral people. We attempt to institutionalize virtue. We recognize that evil exists and it must be confronted and defeated.

Mel Glass, John Keenan and Frank Hogan made decisions

that were morally inspired. They embodied and personified the spiritual essence of American exceptionalism.

The path they placed me on was paved with principle and integrity that led to justice. That's the stuff, the foundational basis, upon which a "Ministry of Justice" is constructed. For granting me this invaluable experience, I am, and will be, forever grateful.

NOTE

The following names of individuals have been changed
and are not their real names:

Vic Arena
Louie Ayala
Frank Backer
Mack Dollinger
Alma Estrada
Ricky Getz
Liam Gynt
Harry Hart
Jennifer Holley
James Hosty
Tim Krupa
Harold Lasky
Lenny Meyers
Tommy Micelli
Abbe Mills (Abbe Romano)
Dr. Morris
Katherine "Kate" Olsen (Fagen)
Peter
Dr. Lucille St. Helme

Index

INDEX

INDEX